Sep 2004

THE
SPORT SCIENCE OF ELITE JUDO ATHLETES

A REVIEW & APPLICATION FOR TRAINING

By Wayland J. Pulkkinen B.P.E., M.Sc., C.K.

THE SPORT SCIENCE OF ELITE JUDO ATHLETES — A REVIEW & APPLICATION FOR TRAINING
By Wayland J. Pulkkinen, B.P.E., M.Sc., C.K.

First Published in 2001 by Pulkinetics Inc.
89 Surrey Street East, Guelph, Ontario, Canada N1H 3P7 www.pulkinetics.com

Distributed by Hatashita Enterprises
Editing and History of Judo by Matt Carter
Judo Photography courtesy of Bob Willingham
Exercise Photography by Dan Banko
Printing by LithoSource Inc. (Toronto, Canada)
Design by Doug Lawless

National Library of Canada Cataloguing in Publication Data

Pulkkinen, Wayland J. (Wayland John), 1967–
The Sport Science of Elite Judo Athletes: A Review & Application for Training

Includes bibliographical references.
ISBN 0–9688693–0–0

1. Judo—Training   1. Title
GV1114.P84 2001   796.815'2   C2001–900394–3

CONTENTS

ACKNOWLEDGEMENTS

This project would not have been possible without the influence, support and encouragement of some individuals, who through their involvement in my life, contributed in some fashion to my physical, mental and spiritual development in Kodokan Judo. These individuals, in no specific order are: Mr. William Doherty (6th dan), Mr. Mitchel Kawasaki (6th dan), Mr. Mike Flynn (4th dan), Mr. Wayne Erdman (6th dan), Mr. Robert J. Zettl (5th dan), Mr. Kevin Kennedy (3rd dan), Mr. Sven Petzchler (3rd dan), Mr. Mike Heney (3rd dan), Mr. Roman Hatashita (4th dan), Mr. Kevin West (5th dan), Mr. Andrew Durand (2nd dan), Mr. Pasi Lauren (4th dan), Ms. Sandra Greaves (5th dan) and Mr. Matt Carter (2nd dan).

Special acknowledgement goes to my parents, Robert and Dianne Pulkkinen; my sister Mya Rajamaki; my uncle, Mr. David Pulkkinen; my sponsor, Mr. Stan Herman; my wrestling coaches, Mr. Nick Cipriano, and Mr. Frances Clayton.

This book is dedicated to my wife, Caroline Frances Adams, who supported me throughout my athletic and academic career, and who selflessly gave of herself to assist me during these endeavours.

PREFACE AND INTRODUCTION

The Olympic sport of Judo has experienced incredible success worldwide since the inception of the martial art in 1882. The current ruling sport body of judo, the International Judo Federation (IJF), governs a membership of millions worldwide of both adults and children practicing the art and sport of judo. In many countries, judo is part of educational curriculums, and follows the trend initiated by its founder and professor of physical education, Dr. Jigoro Kano. Since judo's introduction to the Olympics in 1964, many countries have concentrated efforts on studying the science behind the sport of judo. The majority of these academic investigations have occurred in Europe, particularly Eastern Europe, where sport science is an integral part of coaching and athlete preparation. Not surprisingly, only recently has the western part of the world (North and South America) put efforts into understanding the science of judo. These investigations range from quantifying and identifying the physical make up of the judo athlete to understanding and measuring their psychological performance in both training and competition. Modern day coaching programs in all parts of the world are increasingly turning to the sport scientist in an effort to improve on athletic performance in elite level judo events.

The present document is a collection and review of sport science literature on judo training, performance and athletes. It is not, however, a book on judo competition technique, but rather a comprehensive literature review on sport science as it applies to elite judo performance. It will examine the multifaceted approach to sport science in an attempt to identify what traits are characteristic of elite judo athletes. The majority of the documents cited are collected from academic journals of medicine and sport, and will focus on the physiological, biochemical and psychological adaptations and traits to physical training as it specifically relates to judo performance. It will then examine the effects of overtraining and rapid weight loss; two areas that significantly impact both the training and competition performance of the elite judo athlete and strategies in recognizing and overcoming the effects of each. The final section of the book will present an example of some more common training methods with the aim of achieving the desired physiological, biochemical and psychological adaptations previously discussed. It will conclude with a sample annual training plan, incorporating all the previously discussed components.

A BRIEF HISTORY OF JUDO
FROM THE MEIJI PERIOD TO THE
PRESENT DAY

The Meiji Period (1868–1912) of Japanese history was an era of immense change. Japan had closed its doors to the West some two centuries earlier under the power of the ruling Shogunate, and as a result remained virtually unchanged both politically and industrially, during this period. It was after a number of unsuccessful attempts by Western nations to establish trade with the Japanese during the mid-nineteenth century that the United States finally managed to gain a foothold at the Dutch maintained trading post of Deshima in Nagasaki. This occurred as a result of two notable expeditions: the first by Commodore James Biddle in 1846, and the second by Commodore James Glynn in 1849. The arrival of Commodore Matthew Perry, however, in 1853 permanently set the wheels of change in motion. Perry brought word from then U.S. President, Millard Fillmore, demanding that Japan establish trading and diplomatic relations between the two nations. Fillmore also threatened the use of force if these terms were not met. A treaty of amity was signed the following year between the U.S. and Japan, effectively ending the isolation from the West, which had lasted since 1639. Similar treaties followed with Britain, France, Russia, and the Netherlands, thus beginning Japan's rapid modernization.

Writings by Kano are defined as (front rt. to lt.) 'Jita Kyoei'—Mutual Welfare and Benefit and 'Seriyoku Zenyo'—Effective use of Spirit and Energy

Modernization brought with it the need to adopt many Western conventions. These included: a Western style constitutional government, a new capitalistic outlook, and the development of Western technology. At first glance, it might appear that this process of modernization was a one-way street, with Japan receiving and the West giving, however this was not always the case. Many Japanese traveled to Europe and America to study, and conversely, many Westerners came to Japan to study and teach. Through this exchange system, many aspects of Japanese culture were brought to the West. Japanese aesthetics, art, and architecture were some of the things appreciated by those in the West. Another of these 'gifts' brought to the West was judo. Judo was originally introduced to Europe and America at the turn of the century, and has since become a highly popular, international Olympic sport. The International Judo Federation, founded in 1951, now boasts well over 180 national member federations, and is still growing.

In order for one to fully understand judo, it is important to know where judo came from, and where its roots lie. Judo evolved from the ancient Japanese art of jujutsu. While the exact origins of jujutsu are somewhat of a mystery, most historians tend to agree on certain chronicled events regarding jujutsu. The most popular theory has to do with a battle of strength between two men, Nominosukune and Taimono Kehaya, which occurred during the reign of Emperor Suijin (A.D. 249–280). This battle was an arduous affair involving various grappling and hand-to-hand combat techniques. The eventual victor was Nominosukune, who defeated his opponent by kicking him to death. The result of this contest was the formation of two distinct schools of combat; one developed into modern day sumo wrestling, the other into jujutsu. Through centuries of actual battlefield experience, jujutsu became a highly effective means of attack and defense for the samurai of Japan.

It was not until the Sengoku period (1477–1603), also known as the 'Age of Wars', that the techniques of jujutsu began to be taught at different schools or 'ryu'. Each school focused on its own unique form of jujutsu. One of the first ryu to gain widespread fame throughout Japan was the Takeuchi ryu, which originated in 1532. In a famous fight, a member of the Takeuchi ryu successfully defeated a much larger opponent, thus demonstrating the obvious effectiveness of jujutsu as a form of hand-to-hand combat. Many other schools developed during the Sengoku and Tokugawa (1604–1868) periods. Among the more famous of these schools were the Yoshi ryu, Jikishin ryu, Kito ryu, and the Tenshin-Shinyo ryu.

Dr. Jigoro Kano, the founder of Kodokan Judo.

In 1860, Jigoro Kano, the founder of judo, was born in Miyage in Yamagata prefecture. Kano was said to be a man of 'weak constitution', and took up jujutsu in hopes of strengthening his mind and body. Kano studied many forms of jujutsu and in 1878, he became a student of the Tenshin-Shinyo ryu under the instruction of Masters Hachinosuke Fukuda and Masatomo Iso. He also studied the techniques of the Kito ryu under Master Tsunetoshi Ikubo. Kano continued his diligent study of jujutsu, eventually perfecting his own techniques to which he gave the name, Nippon den Kodokan Judo, in its shortened form, Judo. 'Ju' comes from the Japanese rendering of a Chinese word meaning 'gentle' or 'supple', and is related to the notion of giving way to an opponents strength rather than resisting it. 'Do' means 'way' or 'path', as opposed to 'jutsu' which means 'art'. In so naming judo, Kano wished to distinguish his new school from those of jujutsu. Kano wrote that, 'Jujutsu ryu employed dangerous practices such as throwing by quite incorrect methods or by applying torsion to the limbs.' In judo, Kano wished to create a sport that could be practiced and enjoyed by all, while, at the same time, remaining physically challenging and competitive.

In 1882, at the age of twenty-three and while still a student at Tokyo's Imperial University, Jigoro Kano opened a school for his 'judo'. He called this school the Kodokan, literally meaning, 'place for studying the way'. The original Kodokan was located in Shitaya and had only twelve mats (3' x 6' each) and nine students. When Jigoro Kano passed away in 1938, at the age of 78, there were over 100,000 black belts in judo. There are now millions of black belts registered at the modern Kodokan in downtown Tokyo. The Kodokan is now also the headquarters of the All Japan Judo Federation and is a mecca for judo players around the world. The eight-story building includes a museum, weight training facilities, dormitories and six separate dojo's, with the main dojo holding over 400 mats.

Jigoro Kano was a very well educated man; he spoke English fluently, was headmaster of two prominent Japanese schools, and was an accomplished writer. As a scholar, Kano achieved the title of Professor and became the president of the faculty of Physical Education at the prestigious Tokyo University. Starting in 1911, educational institutions throughout Japan began including judo as part of their curriculum.

In order to further promote judo worldwide, Kano made numerous trips overseas. He visited Britain in 1920, and the United States in 1932 as the honorary president of the Japanese Amateur Athletic Federation at the Olympic Games in Los Angeles. Kano also helped found the Japanese Olympic Committee and attended the International Olympic Conference in Cairo in 1938, in hopes of fulfilling his dream of having judo recognized as an Olympic sport. Sadly, Professor Kano died at sea while returning from the conference. Although in a fitting tribute to the founder of judo, Kano's dream was finally realized when the Games were held in Tokyo in 1964, and judo was made an official Olympic sport.

Europe received its first exposure to jujutsu in 1899, when Yukio Tani (1881–1951) and his brother arrived in England to teach jujutsu at the request of a Mr. B.B. Barton-Wright. More Japanese arrived at the turn of the century, and through numerous demonstrations and exhibitions, jujutsu became very popular in

The Kodokan Judo Institute in Tokyo, Japan.

Britain. It was not until 1918, however, that the first official judo club was founded in Europe. In January of 1918, Gunji Koizumi (1885–1965) opened the Budokwai dojo in London. The Budokwai was originally a Japanese community centre and was frequented by members of the Japanese Imperial Army and Navy and their families who were stationed in London. Although the Budokwai was a judo club, judo was still often referred to as jujutsu in the early 1900's. It was not until 1920, that the word 'judo' actually became widespread.

Koizumi, who is often referred to as the 'father of British judo', was born in Ibaraki prefecture, some twenty miles north of Tokyo. Like Kano before him, Koizumi was an accomplished martial artist. He began studying kenjutsu ('the art of the sword'), when he was only twelve years old. He later studied at the Tenshin-Shinyo ryu under Master Nobushige Tago. In 1904, Koizumi traveled to Fusen, Korea where he studied at a school run by an ex-samurai named Nobukatsu Yamada. Yamada taught him the techniques of the Shin-Shin ryu; jujutsu, and katsu. Two years later, in 1906, Koizumi moved to Singapore where he studied the 144 techniques of the Akijima ryu. In May of the same year, Gunji Koizumi arrived in England and began teaching jujutsu in Liverpool, before opening the London Budokwai in 1918.

Unfortunately, due to the British Museum being extensively damaged in World War II during the Blitz on London, many of the records related to the early history of judo in Britain have been destroyed. Nevertheless, the introduction of judo in Britain helped the spread of judo throughout the rest of Europe, particularly in France, Germany and Holland. On the other side of the Atlantic, Yoshiaki Yamashita, who was a student of Jigoro Kano, introduced judo to America in 1902. Yamashita came to the United States at the request of President Theodore Roosevelt, who had previously learned judo under the instruction of Yamashita while in Japan.

Judo developed slowly in the United States, with dojo's opening primarily on the west coast and in Hawaii. As mentioned previously, Jigoro Kano visited the U.S. in 1932 while attending the Olympic Games and it was during this visit that four 'yudanshakai' (black belt organizations) were formed. These were located in Southern California, Northern California, Seattle, and Hawaii. American judo received a strong boost following the Second World War as many servicemen who had been stationed in Japan had studied judo at the Kodokan and upon their return to the U.S., set up judo clubs of their own.

The introduction of judo to Canada also occurred on the west coast. In 1924, a young Japanese judoka by the name of Takagaki opened Canada's first dojo. The opening of this dojo served both sport and social purposes. Jigoro Kano eventually visited Vancouver and named the Canadian dojo the Kidokan. During the second world war, many Japanese Canadians were forced to relocate east of the Rockies and as a result, judo was spread eastward. After the war ended, many Japanese chose to remain in their new communities and this led to the beginning of judo in places such as Alberta, Toronto and Montreal.

By the 1950's, judo was well established in North America and Europe. In 1956, the inaugural World Judo Championships were held in Tokyo, Japan. At the second World Championships in 1958, one of the pioneers of judo in Ontario, Canada,

The symbol for the International Judo Federation (IJF), the current ruling body of judo.

Masatoshi Umetsu, represented Canada. At this time, judo had not yet implemented weight categories and as a result, there was only one division to be contested for. The domination of the Japanese was apparent at the first two World Championships, but at the third World's held in Paris in 1961, a new champion emerged; the giant Dutchman, Anton Geesink, who also went on to win the first ever Olympic gold medal in judo in 1964.

In the decades to follow, the Japanese continued to reign supreme in the judo world, although recently the tide has shifted. Judo is now, more than ever, a truly international sport. World and Olympic champions have come from virtually all of the major European countries, as well the United States and Brazil and many smaller nations such as Cuba and Yugoslavia. At the 2000 Sydney Olympic Games, Montreal native, Nicolas Gill, won a silver medal in the -100kg division. This compliments his bronze medal from the 1992 Olympics in Barcelona, and his medals from the 1993 and 1999 World Judo Championships, showing that Canada too, is making a name for itself in the Judo World.

Although it can be said that judo is now a truly international sport, it still retains much of its Japanese heritage. Wherever judo is practiced throughout the world, its terminology and customs remain Japanese. Upon entering and leaving a dojo, a judo-ka bows to a portrait of Professor Jigoro Kano as a sign of respect for the man who created this unique sport. Thus, with the many Western ideas and products that have been brought into Japan since the Meiji Restoration (some more freely than others), it is comforting to know that the Japanese have given many 'gifts' to the West in return. Judo is one of the more precious of these.

PART ONE
THE PHYSIOLOGICAL COMPOSITION
OF ELITE JUDO ATHLETES

An Analysis of Judo Mechanics and the Competitive Judo Match

Movement patterns within judo require competitors to grapple the judo uniforms (gi) via the lapel, collar and/or sleeve in order to off-balance (kuzushi) each other enough to execute a throw. Sparring either occurs in standing or ground situations, depending upon individual athlete strategy and the natural development of the match. In standing competition, points are awarded based on the degree of skill demonstrated in a takedown (throw), and range from a take-down to the backside (koka) to a high amplitude throw flat to the back (ippon). In contrast, ground competition points are also awarded for the length of time a pin is executed for a minimum of 10 seconds (koka) to a maximum of 25 seconds (ippon). Furthermore, a automatic victory is awarded when a submission hold is executed via a strangulation or joint manipulation, whereby the opponent either voluntarily submits or is unable to continue competition (ie. becomes unconscious or injured). Thus, immediate victory can be achieved through the awarding of a full-point or 'ippon' in either standing or ground strategies. The relative contribution of standing to ground sparring essentially is determined by the strategies of each athlete. Different tactics will be employed by different judoka depending on individual strengths and weaknesses.

Three officials operate on the mat surface, with the primary decisions made by the acting referee under the observations of two judges concomitantly. All calls must have the support of at least 2 of the 3 officials in order for them to be passed, therefore the two sideline judges may overrule an acting referee if an incorrect call is made. Rules and regulations governing judo by the International Judo Federation (IJF) require athletes to be extremely dynamic throughout the match, and thus, athletes are penalized if they become non-combative and/or defensive during the match. In addition, athletes are also penalized if they voluntarily flee the caution zone of the mat surface in an attempt to avoid an attack. Thus the rules require judo to involve repeated high intensity attacks, and therefore dictate the physiological requirements of each athlete.

The Physical Basis of Competitive Judo: Match Dynamics

In order to understand the metabolic and physiological requirements of judo training, a time motion analysis of the competitive match must be completed. The analysis will enable the sport scientist to evaluate the relative energy system contribution during judo activity. Through this approach, optimal training programs will be able to be individualized, thus prescribing ideal intensity and duration of judo activity for training purposes. Most time motion analysis studies and corresponding research have been done on Olympic wrestling, which is similar in the physiological demand and energy cost as Olympic judo. Competitive Olympic wrestling exists in two forms: free-style and Greco-Roman. Although, it has been demonstrated that there are no physiological differences between wrestlers of both free-style and Greco-Roman styles (Horswill et al, 1992). Freestyle wrestling is characteristic of short duration, high intensity, intermittent exercise lasting a total duration of six minutes (2 three minute bouts). This time may be expanded to three minutes, if the two opponents have a tied score, or either wrestler is absent of a three point lead. Therefore, a match may last anywhere from several seconds, to a maximum of six minutes. Anaerobic power is crucial due to the scoring system for both free-style and Greco-Roman wrestling, using explosive techniques which may end the match prior to regulation time (Horswill et al, 1992). Time motion analysis has demonstrated that Olympic (62 kg) wrestlers perform a mean of 16 (3.0–19.5) high intensity action-reaction sequences. Each attack sequence lasts approximately 3.1 seconds (1–8) in duration, with a mean recovery period of 23.6 seconds (Cipriano, 1993). The recovery period involves submaximal work, primarily utilizing pushing, pulling and lifting actions, from which the wrestler can receive short term recovery, as well as time to prepare for a following attack. As a result, competitive wrestling activity is extremely dynamic in nature, encompassing repeated explosive movements at a high intensity that alternates with sub-maximal work. Thus the primary energy systems utilized are the anaerobic ATP-CP and lactic systems, in the scope of the aerobic system.

Gripping activity as seen in world class contest judo.

In comparison, Olympic judo is a dynamic, physically demanding sport, requiring a high level of physical conditioning and strength in order to be successful and offset fatigue. Many authorities characterize sport judo as an explosive power sport, requiring tremendous reserves of anaerobic power and capacity, yet operating within a well developed aerobic system (Callister et al, 1991; NCCP, 1990; Sharp et al, 1987; Thomas et al, 1989; Takahashi, 1992). Judo is characteristic of short duration, high intensity, intermittent exercise lasting a total match period of five minutes for males and four minutes for females. Therefore, it is primarily an anaerobic sport, consisting of all out bursts of activity ranging from a mean time of approximately 10 to 30 seconds of work to 10 to 15 seconds of rest (NCCP, 1990). This would equate to a work to rest ratio of approximately 2:1 or 3:1. The recovery period often involves submaximal work, primarily performing grappling or gripping actions between each successive attack sequence. This period allows for a shorter term of recovery, as well as time to prepare for a following attack. Sikorski et al (1987) categorized periods of contest judo work into four stages: 0–10 seconds, 11–20 seconds, 21–30 seconds and more than 30 seconds. The highest frequency of rest or breaks (80%) lasted in the 0–10 seconds range, with the highest frequency of activity (39%) in the 11–21 seconds range. Furthermore, Sikorski et al (1987) found the mean time of work activity does not exceed 25 seconds, with a rest period of no more than 10 seconds. Attacks are often initiated within every 10 to 15 seconds of the match. Based on these findings, it can be concluded that the primary source of energy contribution in contest judo is derived from anaerobic glycolysis (Sikorski et al, 1987).

Analysis of World Championships (1981, 1983, 1985); European Championships (1982, 1984, 1985); and Polish Championships (1983, 1984, 1985) by Sikorski et al (1987) illustrates both the frequency and effectiveness of techniques applied by successful elite judoists. Results were derived from examining all seven male divisions, with a minimum sample size of 54 athletes in each category. In all three competitions, there was a higher frequency of attacks and a higher frequency of effectiveness of attacks in the first and last minute of a match. Furthermore, light weight categories (-60 kg, -65 kg, -71 kg) tended to initiate attacks more frequently within a 10 second time period, with heavier divisions attacking within a 15 second time period. Surprisingly, the most effective tactical action was penalizing the opponent for passivity in attack. Lighter divisions (-60, -65 and -71 kg) tended to utilize more hand group throws (ie. seoi-nage), which was in contrast to heavier divisions (-78,-86, -95, +95 kg) that utilized more leg group throws (ie. uchi-mata, o-soto-gari) and performed pins more successfully. Overall, the techniques most often applied during contest judo were seoi-nage, o-soto-gari, uchi-mata and ko-uchi-gari.

Analysis of the 1992 Olympic Games in Barcelona substantiates the time constraints of each division. For males, the range for mean match times (minutes:seconds) were lowest with the +95 kg (2:52) to highest with -86 kg division (3:26). Total mean match time for all seven male divisions were 3:00, with a deviation of 20.7 seconds. Female mean match times were very similar to males, with the lowest time for -72 kg (2:39) to the highest mean time for -66 kg (3:04). Total mean match time for females were 2:54, with a deviation of 8.6 seconds. Combined male and female mean match times were 2:57, with a deviation of 3.9 seconds. When examining recent patterns in elite competitions, we see that there is an increasing trend on victories through penalizing one's opponent through non-combativity.

MALE MEAN MATCH TIMES FROM MAJOR COMPETITIVE EVENTS (IJF, 2001).

Competition Event	Average Match Time	Percent (%) Ippon	Percent (%) Nage Waza	Percent (%) Katame Waza	Percent (%) Other	Percent (%) Non-combat
1995 Worlds	3:43	55.0	45.3	11.0	43.7	36.0
1996 Olympics	3:42	60.1	46.6	5.2	48.2	35.7
1997 Olympics	3:36	17.8	50.5	4.7	44.7	37.4
1999 Worlds	3:31	61.8	48.3	4.1	47.6	31.3
2000 Worlds (Jr.)	3:01	52.7	53.1	4.2	42.7	30.7
Sum	17:55	247.4	243.8	29.2	226.9	171.1
Mean	3:30	49.5	48.8	5.84	45.4	34.2
Std. Dev.	17.24	18.1	3.1	2.92	2.4	3.0

FEMALE MEAN MATCH TIMES FROM MAJOR COMPETITIVE EVENTS (IJF, 2001).

Competition Event	Average Match Time	Percent (%) Ippon	Percent (%) Nage Waza	Percent (%) Katame Waza	Percent (%) Other	Percent (%) Non-combat
1995 Worlds	2:53	47.4	48.3	14.4	37.3	29.9
1996 Olympics	3:06	44.1	55.3	9.3	35.4	23.8
1997 Olympics	3:12	49.4	49.7	9.3	41.0	31.1
1999 Worlds	3:02	48.9	54.2	9.2	36.5	21.9
2000 Worlds (Jr.)	2:55	59.6	60.4	7.2	32.4	20.8
Sum	16:08	249.4	267.9	49.4	182.6	127.5
Mean	3:14	49.9	53.6	9.9	36.5	25.5
Std. Dev.	22.9	5.8	4.8	2.7	3.1	4.7

As we can see, matches can and do end prior to the set time limit in at least 50% of all bouts. This appears to occur at or around the 3 minute mark, with the scoring of 'ippon' or full point awarded to the victor. An interesting trend is the significance and the strategy in penalizing one's opponent for passivity or lack of aggression. This is often seen in the practice of 'kumi kata' or during the process of 'gripping' the opponents uniform. In competition judo, a secure 'grip' can be very advantageous in successfully executing a takedown or throw, and often is the main determining factor in whether an executed attack becomes a winning attack. The practical application of this understanding should be to include this type of physical preparation in the training room. Exercises should focus on developing the flexor muscles of the arm and forearm in addition to sustaining both isotonic and isokinetic contractions for brief periods (5–15 seconds) repeatedly in order to develop both familiarity with fatigue and lactate tolerance in the muscles involved. Tactically, gripping should encompass a means of which the athlete can switch and be versatile with their attack in order to change, counter or combine with other subsequent attacks. Our time motion analysis clearly indicates and validates the energy cost of judo performance. Thus one can conclude that the primary energy systems utilized are the anaerobic ATP-CP and lactic systems, within the scope of the aerobic system.

Physiological Profiles of Elite Judo Athletes

Competitive judo performance utilizes both aerobic and anaerobic energy systems. Physical training for judo competitions emphasizes focusing on both aerobic and anaerobic systems. This section will outline some fundamental adaptations to training, in addition to examining the physiological components of percent body fat, fiber type, aerobic and anaerobic traits of judo athletes from various national teams.

Percent Body Fat of Elite Judo Athletes

Both the IJF (International Judo Federation) and the IOC (International Olympic Committee) regulations require athletes to compete in set weight categories. Competitors are matched by weight divisions, thus athletes demonstrate relatively low levels of body fat with a high strength to mass ratio (Takahashi, 1992). Taylor et al (1981) initially determined body fat values for male Canadian athletes to have a mean value of 12.27%. This was consistent when compared to British male athletes, whose body fat values were reported at 12.3% (Sharp and Koutedakis, 1987). Thomas et al (1989) reported male Canadian athletes to range from 6.7% to 15.8%, with a mean of 9.3%. These findings were similar to those by Callister et al (1991), who demonstrated mean body fat values for American male athletes to be 8.3%, with a standard deviation of 1.0. In all three cases, percent body fat was determined via skin fold thickness. It has been suggested that percent body fat may be a discriminator for success. Callister et al (1991) found that more successful male athletes (those with more international success or competition points) maintained lower body fat percentages. Although this may be true, it may just be a reflection of physiological adaptations to long-term judo training, in so far as most successful athletes tended to be older with greater experience. Nevertheless, judo athletes must maintain an ideal body weight and according to IJF rules, weigh in the morning of the competitive event. Thus weight management and corresponding weight loss is a significant factor in determining success of the judo athlete.

Fibre Type Composition of Elite Judo Athletes

Fibre typing can provide information as to the long-term training adaptations of judo athletes, however, few sources have examined muscle fibre types of elite judo athletes. A study by Callister et al (1991) sampled muscle tissue from vastus lateralis of male and female U.S. judo athletes. Myosin ATPase activity was used to determine fibre types histochemically on 12 µm thick cross sections. Results indicated that females demonstrated a higher mean value contribution of type I (48.9%) than males (35.7%). Furthermore, females had fewer type IIB mean values (10.5%) than males (26.8%), although, type IIA fibres were similar between males (37.1%) and females (38.5%). These results indicate the anaerobic contribution of judo activity. For males, the distribution of fibre types appears to be somewhat evenly displaced, with greater emphasis placed on type IIA. The practical application to the coach and sport scientist is in understanding the metabolic cost of judo activity. Glycolytic muscle fibres (both type IIA and IIB) need to be trained differently and training programs need to reflect this requirement.

Aerobic Requirements of Elite Judo Athletes

The aim of aerobic conditioning in judo is to train and improve the working capacity of the heart and its ability to deliver oxygen to the muscles. It has been suggested that the optimal way to improve the oxygen delivery is continuous training, while interval training is more effective in increasing oxygen utilization (Brooks and Fahey, 1985). Applications to judo performance involve a greater recovery from anaerobic work (via lactate metabolism), in addition to a faster re-synthesis of phosphate. By far, the marker of aerobic performance is the calculation of an individuals maximal oxygen uptake (VO_2). This process is the highest oxygen uptake the individual can attain during exercise lasting longer than 2 minutes at a maximal intensity (Astrand and Rodahl, 1986). Research indicates that aerobic training can increase VO_2 by 15–20 %. (NCCP, 1990). The biochemical and metabolic adaptations that occur with endurance training are an increase in glycolytic enzymes (LDH, PDH, PFK), beta oxidation enzymes (acyl carnitine transferase), as well as increases in citrate synthetase in the TCA cycle. The primary benefit of these physiological changes are due to a greater use of fatty acids via beta oxidation for metabolic energy, thus reducing the demand for glycogen via glycolysis (Astrand and Rodahl, 1986). This in turn will provide a 'glycogen sparring' effect, therefore prolonging the time it takes to fatigue during strenuous exercise. Applications of aerobic conditioning to judo involves a greater recovery from anaerobic work (via removal of metabolic biproducts), in addition to a faster re-synthesis of phosphate (NCCP, 1990). This ability to recover quickly is crucial between matches, as that the number of matches performed during a tournament may range as high as 6 to 8 in one day.

Although aerobic power is an essential component of judo physiology, current literature indicates that the VO_2 values for elite judo athletes are higher than normal, but not as high as endurance athletes. In comparison, endurance athletes, like marathon runners and cross-country skiers, typically demonstrate VO_2 values of 70–80 $ml.kg^{-1}.min^{-1}$. Taylor et al (1981) initially tested male Canadian judo athletes, and found mean VO_2 values to be at 57.5 $ml.kg^{-1}.min^{-1}$. Thomas et al (1989) examined VO_2 values of Canadian male judo athletes, and compared these mean values to other nations. Canadian judoists were determined to have a mean value of 59.2 $ml.kg^{-1}.min^{-1}$, with values ranging from 49.7–65.2 $ml.kg^{-1}.min^{-1}$. This was similar to findings reported by Little (1991), who found that mean VO_2 values for senior male judo athletes were 53.75 $ml.kg^{-1}.min^{-1}$. When compared to Australian, Polish and Norwegian judo athletes, VO_2 values were reported at 53.2, 59.0 and 58.5 $ml.kg^{-1}.min^{-1}$, respectively. Findings by Mickiewicz et al (1987) revealed VO_2 values of elite judo senior and junior males, and senior female Polish athletes to be 60.22, 60.23, and 49.90 $ml.kg^{-1}.min^{-1}$, respectively. Callister et al (1991) determined U.S.

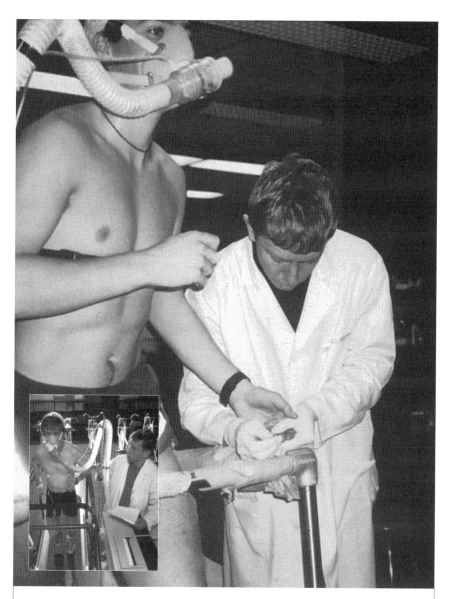

Physiological testing and monitoring is a crucial part of designing any training program.

male athletes to have a mean VO_2 value of 55.6 ml.kg^{-1}.min^{-1}, with females at 52.0 ml.kg^{-1}.min^{-1}. In comparison, peak VO_2 values for elite wrestlers range between 60 to 70 ml.kg^{-1}.min^{-1} (Cipriano, 1993). These values are higher than those cited by Horswill et al (1992), who reported peak VO_2 to range form 51 to 62 ml.kg^{-1}.min^{-1}, although, differences in peak values may be due to the format of assessment (ie. tread-mill tests vs. arm and leg ergometry). It was reported that VO_2 relative to body size was inversely related to weight division for both males and females respectively. This was identical to what Thomas et al (1989) found, in that aerobic power relative to body size tended to decrease with increases in weight divisions. This may be as a result of a greater proportion of body fat in the larger athletes.

Practical applications to the coach and sport scientist involve an understanding that aerobic performance and conditioning is not paramount in the physical development of world class judo athletes. Judo performance requires a good aerobic base or aerobic working capacity, and this can be developed through the nature of a typical competition practice. Judo practice would be a means of improving general conditioning, whereas running would be a means of enhancing general conditioning (Matsumoto et al, 1978). The very nature of judo training would involve athletes performing at or above 75% of their individual heart rate maximums for a sustained period of 30–40 minutes during free practice sparring or 'randori' (Kaneko et al, 1978). Perhaps the greatest benefit of aerobic training is the judo athlete's ability to operate at a high percent of their individual aerobic capacity. Research has indicated that trained aerobic individuals can work at 75–85% of their aerobic power before experiencing fatigue (NCCP, 1990). Callister et al (1991) reported that ventilatory thresholds of judo athletes were high, and that lactate levels following treadmill testing were low. This was most likely due to a reflection of the large quantity of high intensity training performed by elite judo athletes. This introduces the concept of anaerobic threshold training (AnT), or the point at which lactate production exceeds its removal during exercise (Astrand and Rodahl, 1986). Due to the high intensity nature of the sport, judo athletes repeatedly operate at or above the AnT throughout the course of training and competition. As a result, training should involve competitive situations, which would require the athlete to attain their individual AnT for a brief period. The corresponding physiological and biochemical adaptations would result in the athlete being able to perform at a higher percent of his VO_2, and thus perform with more intensity during the match, in addition to being able to recover quicker between each high intensity match. The judo athlete should be tested regularly throughout the year to determine if the individual's VO_2 score is at a comparable level to other world class judo athletes. Scores should be at a minimum of 55–60 ml.kg^{-1}.min^{-1}, and if not, focus on the early stages of training should be to ensure that this score is acquired. Successful participation in judo competitions is technical mastery supported with above average endurance capacities (Little, 1991). This is typically done early in the athlete's career prior to world level competition and often is a result or bi-product of regular repeated practices over several years.

Anaerobic Requirements of Elite Judo Athletes

This energy system involves both the ATP-CP (Alactic) and Lactate (anaerobic glycolysis) systems. As mentioned previously, judo primarily involves the anaerobic system, therefore training specificity is crucial in the adaptation of this system. The following will be a brief review of the mechanics behind the alactic and lactate energy systems. It will focus on two measures commonly used in sport science to evaluate the effectiveness of training programs, and present a profile of what some world class judo athletes are capable of performing. The judo coach must understand what these components are, and how to adjust training regimes to ensure that the appropriate stimuli are present.

Alactic and Lactic Components for Judo Performance

The ability to recover quickly from anaerobic work is essential for competition success, since the total number of matches performed during a tournament may range as high as 6 to 8 bouts (Cipriano, 1993). The alactic system uses creatine phosphate (PCr) to generate intense bursts of action. It is characterized by maximal (100% VO_2) exercise lasting 10 to 15 seconds in duration. The value of this system is its tremendous ability to completely replenish stores after depletion within a period of 2 to 3 minutes of rest (Astrand and Rodahl, 1986). This occurs during periods of maximal exercise lasting approximately 90 seconds in duration. Lactate is produced and transforms to lactic acid from pyruvate. Lactic acid dissociates into a lactate substrate (Lac-) and hydrogen ions (H+), which causes muscle pH to decrease (Astrand and Rodahl, 1986). As a result, there is a corresponding increase in muscle acidity, which causes muscle fatigue due to the accumulation of H+. One possible explanation for this fatigue is due to the inhibition of phosphofructokinase (PFK), which is essential for the production of ATP (Astrand and Rodhal, 1986).

In comparison, the lactate energy system can be defined as anaerobic glycolysis, which is essentially the incomplete breakdown of glycogen in the absence of oxygen (Astrand and Rodahl, 1986). This occurs during periods of maximal exercise lasting approximately 90 seconds in duration. Removal of lactic acid is fairly slow, and requires approximately 15–20 minutes to remove one half of the concentration of lactic acid formed (NCCP, 1990). Metabolic adaptations to lactate training involve increases in glycolytic enzymes (CPK, PFK, LDH), and increases in buffer capacity (due to increased concentrations of bicarbonate). Also included is hypertrophy, as well as smaller increases in both glycogen and creatine phosphate stores. Long-term changes may involve a conversion from type IIA fibres to type IIB (Astrand and Rodahl, 1986). The application to judo performance essentially involves developing the athlete's corresponding tolerance to muscular fatigue (due to increases in metabolic buffers and larger stores of PrC). In addition to this, the athlete will be able to generate higher power outputs for a longer period of time. Due to the nature of the sport, judoists are required to perform repeated spurts of high intensity activity, which in turn would maximize the use of the lactate system. Results from time motion analysis indicate that judo activity requires a range from 10 to 30 seconds for execution, which is within the time constraints for the lactate system.

Perhaps the most important benefit of aerobic conditioning for judo involves improvements in the lactate threshold. The lactate threshold has been defined as the point at which lactate production exceeds lactate removal (Astrand and Rodahl, 1986). The physical nature of competitive judo requires the athlete to sustain power at a high percentage of their individual VO_2 throughout the course of the match. This is obvious when examining the time motion analysis of the judo match and the energy system used in performance. Often, this level of power output would be at or exceed the lactate threshold. Consequently, this would produce high levels of blood lactate, which would in turn promote premature fatigue and ineffective execution of techniques throughout the match. The application to sport performance essentially involves developing the athlete's corresponding tolerance to muscular fatigue. Due to the nature of the sport, judo athletes are required to perform repeated spurts of high intensity activity, which in turn would maximize the use of the lactate system. The adaptations that occur will be a relatively small increase in the concentration of PCr stores within the muscle, although, most of the benefit occurs from an increase in intracellular enzyme concentration. This will assist with a prolonged use of the ATP-CP system as opposed to a pre-mature use of the lactic system. The end result is the athlete's improved ability to perform at a higher percent of his VO_2, and thus perform with more intensity and effectiveness in execution of technique.

Anaerobic Power and Capacity of Elite Judo Athletes

Some sources have examined the anaerobic power and capacity of elite judo athletes. Evaluations are typically made by standard Wingate Anaerobic Tests at a set resistance based on the athlete's weight for either legs or arms. Anaerobic capacity is determined by the mean power output throughout a 30 second test. This reflects combined alactic and lactic energy systems. Peak power is determined by the highest power output achieved at any five second period of the test. This is specific to the alactic energy system, and reflects the availability of creatine phosphate stores. Measurements of power are expressed in Watts per kilogram ($W.kg^{-1}$), and as Joules per kilogram ($J.kg^{-1}$). Taylor et al (1989) revealed that lower body anaerobic peak power and capacity of male Canadian judo athletes were evaluated at a mean of 13.7 $W.kg^{-1}$ and 320 $J.kg^{-1}$, respectively. Furthermore, mean values for upper body anaerobic peak power and capacity were determined at 11.3 $W.kg^{-1}$ and 260 $J.kg^{-1}$, respectively.

In comparison, Olympic wrestlers have been shown to have peak anaerobic power at 6.1 to 7.5 $W.kg^{-1}$ (Horswill et al, 1992). Studies by Sharp and Koutedakis (1987) examined anaerobic power and capacity in elite gymnasts, rowers and judo athletes. Resistance was set at 8% of the athlete's body weight. Mean weight values for the judoists were 85.0 kg. Upper body mean Wingate values of British judo athletes were found to be 8.5 $W.kg^{-1}$ for capacity, and 10.6 $W.kg^{-1}$ for peak power. These values of capacity and peak power were lower than those of gymnasts (9.5 $W.kg^{-1}$, 11.0 $W.kg^{-1}$) and rowers (10.0 $W.kg^{-1}$, 11.5 $W.kg^{-1}$) respectively. Sharp and Koutedakis (1987) concluded that body weight related resistance may constitute a greater proportion of their absolute muscular strength. This may be in part to the wide fluctuation in body mass of the subjects. These sources both emphasize the importance of developing anaerobic power and capacity in judo athletes. Findings by Mickiewicz et al (1987) are similar when comparing anaerobic capacity of the legs in elite Polish judo athletes. Mean values for senior and junior males were 11.45 and 11.42 W.kg[-1], respectively. Senior female athletes were much lower with a mean value of 9.53 W.kg[-1]. Results of Wingate tests on the arms in the junior athletes were found to be a mean value of 8.79 W.kg[-1]. Mickiewicz et al (1987) stated that maximum power developed with lower extremities in juniors was higher when compared with power developed in upper extremities. The population examined did not differ in results between senior and junior athletes, thus suggesting that anaerobic capacity may not change with level of judo experience. The values obtained from testing are similar to those of other elite anaerobic based athletes, therefore, suggesting some benefit in modifying training regimes. Judo coaches must incorporate regular testing of anaerobic power and capacity in order to compare his athlete's scores to other world calibre athletes. If scores are lower than world level competitors, training should focus on improving anaerobic performance until more acceptable values occur.

Blood Lactate Concentrations of Judo Athletes in Competition and Training

Measurements of blood lactate can reveal the intensity and degree of training adaptation in athletes, and consequently are an effective means in prescribing exercise intensity for training (MacDougall et al, 1992). Some sources have identified the onset of blood lactate accumulation (OBLA) at 4.0 mmol.L, which is the point when lactate accumulates in blood exponentially (Astrand and Rodahl, 1986). Some highly anaerobically trained individuals may have lactate accumulation levels that exceed this standard value, therefore, determining individual lactate profiles from a sport specific test is essential in determining optimal training intensity (MacDougall et al, 1992). Taylor et al (1989) found lactate values of Canadian judo athletes following lower and upper body Wingate tests to be 15.2 and 14.5 mmol.L, respectively. This was somewhat lower than findings by Mickiewicz et al (1987) following Wingate tests for anaerobic capacity. Results of senior males, junior males and senior females following lower body anaerobic capacity tests demonstrated mean values of 19.3, 15.2 and 15.8 mmol.L respectively. Callister et al (1991) periodically measured lactate values for male and female U.S. athletes throughout 3 months of regular training. Measurements followed sparring matches during free practice (randori), and were determined to have mean values of 8.4 and 7.2 mmol.L, respectively. Randori matches were typically 3 minutes in length, followed by approximately 30 seconds of rest. Callister et al (1991) reported that lactate values following 3 to 7 bouts of randori of this fashion typically measured a mean of 9.1 mmol.L. Blood lactate does not appear to decrease between competition matches, even when adequate rest is provided. In fact, lactate values during competition were found to increase with the number of matches completed. Post-match lactate values of Polish judoists competing in the Matsumae Cup (1986) increased from 10.3, 13.3, 15.9, and 17.2 mmol.L following four matches (Sikorski et al, 1987). In comparison, lactate values of Polish athletes at national championships were found to be a mean of 13.7 mmol.L following 5 matches (Sikorski et al, 1987).

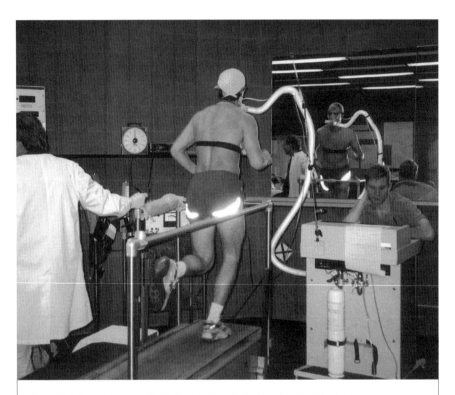

An athlete being tested for blood lactate levels to determine his individual lactate threshold.

The practical application of testing for blood lactate levels throughout the training year is in establishing adequate baseline levels for training. Most elite judo athletes experience very high levels of blood lactate accumulation during training. Many values exceed 8.0 mmol.L, which is double OBLA levels. High blood lactate levels in combination with hypoxia (low O_2 levels) are very effective stimuli for causing the appropriate changes for cellular metabolism. Judo athletes, in particular, would benefit from higher concentrations of oxidative enzymes, thus allowing for higher power outputs. This can directly translate into improved muscle endurance for repeated and sustained muscle contraction needed during a competitive match. In short, the higher the power output, the less fatigue and greater effectiveness of the attack. The judo coach needs to incorporate drills during the training session aimed at improving these parameters. Generally, this type of focus in training would be most beneficial 12 weeks prior to a major competitive event.

Strength Training Principles Applied for Judo Performance
Judo performance requires both strength and muscular endurance for success. Strength can be classified as either absolute strength (total body strength), or explosive strength (power), both of which are required for judo performance (Fisher, 1981). Power maintains a higher slope to peak force, whereas peak force requires a much longer period to reach its plateau. Maximum strength is identified as the force or tension a muscle can exert against a given resistance in maximal effort, while power can be defined as the rate of force development (Sale and MacDougall, 1981). Certain principles for strength training have been identified, which must be followed for optimal adaptation. Sale and MacDougall (1981) outline the key components of strength training for sport. The principle of overloading (increased resistance and/or tension) is necessary to impose a stress stimulus on the muscular system. All exercises must reproduce the sport movement as closely as possible. This principle of specificity of training involves utilizing exercises, which are identical in contraction force, type, velocity and movement pattern of judo movements. Song (1980), identified the four types of muscle contraction as: (i) isometric (tension produced with no change in muscle length); (ii) isotonic (muscle shortens with varying tension while lifting a constant load); (iii) isokinetic (tension produced while shortening at a constant speed through a full range of motion); (iv) eccentric (muscle lengthens while developing tension).

Applications to judo training then would require mainly power exercises, involving concentric contractions at or near maximal resistance as quickly as possible (Takahashi, 1992). Specific muscle groups take precedence in training for judo. Development of the legs, primarily the hip and knee extensors, are of utmost importance in executing basic judo techniques. In addition to leg development, upper body strength of the muscles involved in pulling and pushing are essential for judo performance. Fischer (1981) recommends five basic exercises of: good mornings, leg squats, bench press, bent over barbell rowing and the power snatch, to develop strength. The third principle outlined by Sale and MacDougall (1981) is that of progression, which involves the systematic increase in the resistance load throughout the course of a program. Finally, both volume and frequency define what energy system

Specificity of Strength Training:
Sport specific strength training is essential for developing optimum results.

or what adaptation is being sought after. This is also contingent upon what stage of the training year the athlete is currently involved in. Early phases in training mainly involve increasing absolute strength, while mid-year and later phases of training are concerned with power, speed and endurance development (Verkhoshansky and Lazarev, 1989). The judo athlete must have a well rounded approach to strength training, incorporating both muscular strength and endurance training (Takahashi, 1992). All types of muscular contraction take place throughout the course of judo activity. Adaptations to strength training involve increases in muscle girth (hypertrophy) and cross-sectional area. Also included are enzymatic changes, capillarization changes and increase in motor unit recruitment (Sale and MacDougall, 1981). Improvements in strength will also aid in joint stability and improve flexibility, which will reduce the risk of injury.

Training exercises should attempt to reflect the physical demands of the sport. Furthermore, strength training must be congruent with the energy system being trained for each phase of the yearly training plan. For example, high repetition, circuit type strength exercises should be trained at the same time that anaerobic judo drills are used. This will develop muscular endurance overall, during the competitive phase of the season. Supplemental strength training serves as a necessary means for judo preparation. It can be done year round, as long as it corresponds to the physiological demands of each training phase. It is imperative that both the athlete and coach understand that strength training is supplemental to judo specific practice. Furthermore, the very nature of judo training involves a high degree of natural strength training and this must be considered when incorporating strength training in order to avoid overtraining or fatigue.

Strength Profiles of Elite Judo Athletes

Due to the physical demands on the judo athlete during a match, strength is a key component in the success of executing techniques. Taylor et al (1989) evaluated strength performance of male Canadian judo athletes based on left and right handgrip strength, as well as observing a bench press one repetition maximum lift (1RM). Muscular endurance was determined by performing as many repetitions as possible during a bench press at 70% of the individual's 1RM. Mean values for right grip strength were 56.4 kg, and 55.7 kg for left grip strength. Both left and right grip strengths had a standard deviation score of 6.6 kg, and a total combined left and right handgrip value of 112.1. This value was within normal percentile ranges (106–112) when compared with similar aged males of 20 to 29 years. Furthermore, combined mean handgrip scores were higher than those of elite varsity wrestlers in both pre (100.2) and post (102.1) varsity seasons (Cipriano and Song, 1984). Pulkkinen (1992) found combined mean handgrip strength of varsity wrestlers (107.3) to have a significant correlation to anaerobic power. Taylor et al (1989) found mean scores for 1RM bench press was 100 kg., while the mean number of repetitions performed at 70% 1RM was 16, with a standard deviation score of 3 repetitions. This mean 1RM value was higher than those of varsity level wrestlers (98.5 kg.) as reported by Pulkkinen (1992). The difference between judo athletes and wrestlers in handgrip strength is largely due to level of competition and years of training. Furthermore, 1RM as determined by the bench press is largely dependent on the technique of the exercise, which may also explain the higher values in the judo athletes, however, it is worth comparing handgrip values to similar athletic populations in order to develop adequate strength profile. Callister et al (1991) also examined strength of male and female U.S. judo athletes, however, strength was assessed using a Cybex II dynamometer for both knee and elbow flexor and extensor muscles. All subjects were tested during concentric contractions at angular velocities of 60, 90, 180, 240, and 300 degrees. Absolute and relative to body weight torque values were used for comparisons. Results demonstrated that isokinetic strength relative to lean body mass (LBM) was consistently greater for women in the -56 kg and -61 kg divisions. This was similar with -71 kg and -78 kg males demonstrating stronger performance when compared to -60 kg and -65 kg males, except in elbow extensors. The -86 kg and -95 kg males were consistently the weakest when strength was expressed relative to LBM. Callister et al (1991) concluded that these athletes compromised maximizing their individual muscle strength due to frequent weight loss procedures, in addition to the constraints of keeping body weight low. Furthermore, it was suggested that optimal resistance training programs should concentrate on either one of two extremes: a 1–2 RM (repetition maximum) for strength, or 15–20 RM for muscular endurance. Omitting the 5–8 RM range will avoid producing maximal adaptations in hypertrophy, which will increase LBM, as well as total body weight.

It is clear from the following strength profiles that judo athletes require a high capacity to generate maximal strength. Furthermore, physiological testing of strength is necessary in order to establish where the judo athlete is in comparison to other world class judo athletes. Strength training is a crucial part to the development of the elite judo athlete. Consequently, the adaptations required for elite performance often take years of preparation in order to apply strength gains to the specific movements of the sport. Strength development should not take precedence over judo training, but rather serve as a supplement to training.

PART TWO

RAPID WEIGHT LOSS AND OVERTRAINING—
CONCERNS FOR JUDO PERFORMANCE

Preparing the athlete for elite level competition involves a systematic increase in both the volume and intensity of training. The physical and psychological demands require the athlete to travel world wide, attend various training camps, deal with injuries and weight loss, and often, compete in back to back tournament events. Included is the deadline and pressure of meeting both the international and domestic sport governing bodies requirements for both Olympic and World teams. All of this is can add up to a recipe for disaster and expose the athlete to an ever present risk of overtraining. The IJF recognizes seven weight divisions for both male and female judo competitors. Male weight classes are: -60, -66, -73, -81, -90, -100, +100 kg. Female weight classes are: -48, -52, -57, -63, -70, -78, +78 kg. Furthermore, the IJF requires that judo competitors weigh in the morning of the competition event. Many techniques and strategies have been utilized in attempt to minimize both the amount of time necessary to lose a set amount of weight. Often, the international competitor is required to weigh in several times (weekly) throughout a competitive tour due to participation in weekly competitions. As a result, poorly conducted weight loss practices can have an adverse affect on the outcome of the competition. The following section will examine the physiological and psychological consequences of both rapid weight loss and overtraining. It will contrast and compare these conditions to sport performance and the direct effect on the athlete. In so doing, the coach can better understand the corresponding benefits and downfalls of each condition, and adjust their own training regimes as necessary.

Physical Performance and Rapid Weight Loss in Sport

Rapid weight loss is a common practice among amateur wrestlers and judoists. Wrestlers and judo athletes typically compete in a weight class which is 5–10% below their usual weight in an attempt to gain an advantage over their competitors (Brownell et al, 1987; Fogelholm et al, 1993; Tarnopolsky et al, 1996). Although this practice remains to be true, it has been reported that there is little difference between competitive success and the amount of weight lost or gained following weigh-in (Horswill et al, 1994). It has been suggested that more than 90% of competitive wrestlers lose weight, with at least 80% or more engaging in rapid weight losses of 5–10 lbs weekly. Similarly, 86% of judo athletes typically lose 4.0 kg within 15 days of a competition. Furthermore, this practice can occur on average 15 times per season, depending on the tournament requirements and the competitive level of the athlete (Coles, 1999).

FACTS AND FIGURES OF RAPID WEIGHT LOSS & DEHYDRATION

›   done by fluid and food restriction
›   often done 3–5 days of weigh in
›   involves losing 5% or more of body weight
›   need 12 hours to replace 50% of muscle glycogen
›   judo provides 2–3 hours to replace stores following weigh in
›   missing weight is default and penalty
›   causes rebound effect with weight gain

Rapid weight loss procedures usually involve loosing approximately 3–4 kg in 3–4 days prior to weigh-in through a combination of dietary and fluid restrictions. Other methods of weight loss include exercising in heated environments, wearing of rubber suits, spitting, vomiting and the use of laxatives and diuretics have been known to occur (Brownell et al, 1987; Tarnopolsky et al, 1996). Consequently, the accompanying physiological effects produced by this approach are of great concern in order to prepare the athlete for optimal physical performance for the upcoming competition. It has been documented that rapid weight reduction can impair physical performance in aerobic, anaerobic and strength parameters. Specifically, the athlete's ability to perform at a high intensity (endurance capacity) would be adversely affected. This may be attributed to decreases in muscle strength and endurance following rapid weight loss of 4–5% body weight (Mnatzakian and Vaccaro, 1986). Some researchers did not find any difference in physical performance (vertical jump height and/or Wingate performance) following both gradual (3–4 kg in 3–4 weeks) and rapid (3–4 kg in 2–3 days) weight loss (Fogelholm et al, 1993). Nevertheless, effective weight management and corresponding weight loss practice can play a crucial role in the success or failure in competition performance.

Physiological Effects of Dehydration and Rapid Weight Loss
A least 60% of the human body is composed of water, with roughly 2/3 of water in intracellular and 1/3 extracellular such as plasma and lymph (Coles, 1999). Dehydration in mammals causes a decrease in body fluid and an increase in osmolarity. Extreme losses in body fluid can cause disturbances to thermo-regulation and cardiovascular function. The general homeostatic responses in mammals involves decreases in both fecal and renal water loss, reduction in metabolism and also in evaporation and protection of plasma volume (Silanikove, 1994). Dehydration can be defined as the loss of body fluid of 1% or more of body weight. During prolonged

exercise, water loses of 3 L.hr^{-1} have been reported, with more than 90% occurring as a direct result of sweating. The physiological changes that can occur with dehydration involve decreased sweat rate, plasma volume, cardiac output, VO$_2$, work capacity, muscle strength and glycogen concentration (Brooks and Fahey, 1985). Dehydration of 5% or more of body weight can produce lethargy, fatigue and loss of appetite. This produces a disturbed electrolyte balance, which can easily influence the muscle cell's ability to contract and its susceptibility to metabolites (Astrand and Rodahl, 1986). Burge et al (1993) reported that rapid (2 hours) dehydration (5% body weight) caused a significant decrease in physical performance. Specifically, it was demonstrated that plasma volume significantly decreased 12.5% following rapid dehydration of 5% body weight. Fluid loss is rapid at or near the end of the weight loss procedure (last 24–48 hours), and there may not be enough time to shift out of the intracellular space to compensate for the loss from plasma volume and extracellular fluid volume (Tarnopolsky et al, 1996). As a result, judo athletes may not be adequately re-hydrated for competition following the weight loss procedure. Although, some researchers have reported that five hours of re-hydration and muscle glycogen re-synthesis is sufficient to re-store pre-weight loss levels (Tarnopolsky et al, 1996). This redistribution of plasma into working muscles has been reported to affect serum magnesium concentration (Fogelholm et al, 1994). In comparison, weight loss (rapid and gradual) did not appear to effect erythrocyte TKAC (thiamin status), GRAC (riboflavin status), serum ferritin, potassium and zinc concentrations during weight loss procedures. Alterations in E-ASTAC (vitamin B6 status) and serum magnesium concentration were different between weight loss procedures (rapid vs. gradual), thus suggesting negative trends with gradual weight loss.

RAPID WEIGHT LOSS (4–5% IN BODY WEIGHT) CAN:

> effect strength, immune function, aerobic capacity, blood volume and pressure, body temp
> increase resting heart rate, fatigue, mental confusion
> promote an added strain on heart and kidney function
> increase possibilities of injuries
> increase opportunities for a competitor to score

It is documented that with exercise, there is an elevation in core temperature and sweat production (Sawka et al, 1985). Core temperature drives the sweating mechanism, and as a result elevated core temperatures can remain long after exercise recovery (Pivarnik and Wilderson, 1988). It has been suggested that this may be a result of post-exercise evaporative heat loss, as well as a result of hypo-hydration. Sawka et al (1985) demonstrated an increase in rectal temperatures with exercise by 0.15°C for each percent decrease in body weight via sweat loss. Similarly, Pilardeau et al (1988) reported that under unvaried conditions the quantity of sweat produced was related to work load and heart rate. These responses have been reported to be a result from a resultant increase in core temperature, electrolyte and renal changes occurring during sub-maximal exercise (Brownell et al, 1987). Elevated core temperature and resultant dehydration inevitably have an adverse effect on physical performance.

It has been demonstrated that water deficits of 4% can reduce aerobic capacity by 48% and muscular force by 8% (Deschemes and Kramer (1989). This has been studied through the sport of wrestling via a wrestling performance test in order to evaluate the effects of rapid weight loss on wrestling performance. Klinzing and Karpowicz (1986) designed a test protocol requiring subjects complete a series of wrestling techniques at a intensity similar to a wrestling match, which consisted of two 3-minute rounds. This was done before and after a 5% weight loss by self determined means of fluid and food restriction in combination with exercise, which occurred approximately 50 hours prior to testing. Results demonstrated impaired muscular endurance during performance due to an earlier onset of fatigue.

Reduced carbohydrate and protein intake over a period (ie. 3–4 weeks) can produce losses in protein and glycogen concentrations. Inadequate consumption of protein in the diet during weight loss conditions produce low levels of plasma amino acids (glutamine), which is associated with chronic fatigue and infection in judo athletes following heavy training (Kingsbury et al, 1998). In addition to this, it has also been reported that muscle glycogen concentration has shown to remain 38% below pre-weight loss baseline levels even after 3 hours of carbohydrate and fluid consumption. Klinzing and Karporwicz (1986) concluded that muscle glycogen stores were reduced by 45% following concurrent dehydration and food restriction in wrestlers. Similarly, Tarnopolsky et al (1996) reported that muscle glycogen wet weight significantly decreased 54% following rapid weight loss (5% body weight) in wrestlers over a 3 day period. Following 17 hours of food and fluid repletion (ad libitum), glycogen concentration was 83% of baseline in wrestlers, although glycogen levels did not change significantly following 4 simulated wrestling matches.

Psychological effects of rapid weight loss can lead to increases in confusion, depression, anger, fatigue and tension. Often, repeated periods of weight cycling may lead to a cynical attitude towards sport, thus causing the athlete to withdraw altogether (Coles, 1999). The result is a negative effect on performance and exposure to related psycho-behavioral issues, such as disordered eating. Any sport or activity, which involves monitoring of weight and or body image, has an exposure to disordered eating behaviors. Specifically, male and female wrestlers have been identified as risk groups for disordered eating due to their participation in weight management and practice of binge eating (Coles, 1999). Coaches are often unaware or inexperienced in dealing with issues involving weight loss practices or disordered eating. Furthermore, many international sport or governmental agencies do not have specific guidelines for the practice of weight loss for competition.

In summary, evidence supports that circulatory impairments associated specifically with rapid weight loss and wrestling/judo performance have been shown to cause an overall decrease in physical and even mental performance. The contribution of increased core temperature to this parameter essentially involves the physiological effects of dehydration. Dehydration has been shown to reduce circulation blood volume resulting in a decreased venus return to the heart. Physical working capacity and endurance is significantly reduced leading to an earlier onset of fatigue. Weight loss is a part of judo sport performance and a requirement that the athlete must continually deal with throughout their career. As a result, the coach and athlete must plan for effective weight loss to minimize the negative physiological effects of rapid, illprepared weight loss.

Overtraining: An Introduction

Preparation for high performance sport competition involves periods of high volume training (Vos, Fry and Kraemer, 1992). The difficulty in determining the optimal loads for training, along with adequate recovery and rest, is problematic for both coaches and athletes. Training must be monitored continually to assess whether the stimulus for adaptation is effective. Unfortunately, even in the presence of regular monitoring, training loads can become too excessive, resulting in poor performance.

Several terms have been used to identify states of physical exhaustion. Overreaching is the intentional or unintentional inducement of short term overtraining, the symptoms of which can be reversed by allowing a longer than usual regeneration period (Fry, Morton and Keast, 1992; Vos, Fry and Kraemer, 1992). This typically occurs when an athlete attempts to adapt to training loads that are greater than the body's metabolic processes can deal with. Recovery from overreaching usually involves a few days up to two weeks of rest (Lehmann, Foster and Kuel, 1993). In contrast, Kuipers and Keizer (1988) identified muscular overtraining as transient local fatigue and muscle soreness following exercise that exceeds muscular stress tolerance. Furthermore, Kuipers and Keizer (1988) indicated that this form of overtraining generally occurs after single or repeated bouts of excessive exercise, which promotes structural damage to muscle fibers.

When overloading exceeds recovery and adaptation within a specified time, overtraining or an over-reaching response can occur (Fry, Morton and Keast, 1992; Kuipers and Keizer, 1988). Overtraining syndrome can then be described as the final stage in chronic fatigue states, developing from overreaching (Fry, Morton and Keast, 1992; Vos, Fry and Kraemer, 1992). Recovery typically requires a long-term process, involving biochemical, physiological and psychological parameters returning to normal levels. Budget (1990) indicated that overtraining may be induced by sudden increases in training load such as participating in intensive exercise with short rests and frequent competitions. Some authorities have suggested that weekly increases in training volumes of more than 5 to 10% may induce overtraining (Mackinnon and Hooper, 1991). In addition, other contributing factors such as frequency of competition and travel, intense strength training and year round training with no break between sessions can predispose athletes to overtraining (Mackinnon and Hooper, 1991). Other factors such as the accumulation or deficiency in life stressors, diet, rest, weight loss, occupational and relationship stress also can produce a cumulative effect in predisposing an athlete to overtraining. Procedures for monitoring training stress should involve a multifaceted approach of evaluating the individual's response on physiological, biochemical, psychological and performance variables over a period of time. Assessment of training loads should examine all parameters, which respond to a training stimulus. Only this approach will the coach be able to accurately evaluate effectiveness of the training stimulus, and make necessary amendments when required. Many authorities have indicated that with a decrease in the volume of training or extended breaks lasting one to two weeks, complete recovery from training overstress and performance improvements may occur (Budget, 1990; Fry et al, 1992; Houmard, 1991; Kuipers and Keizer, 1988). In other words, an inability to observe positive changes following rest, indicates that a state of overtraining may exist. Moreover, this period of recovery is necessary to facilitate effective adaptations to the training stimulus, thus permitting the athlete to advance to a higher load.

The General Adaptation Syndrome: A Model of Stress Manifestation

Hans Selye (1956), examined the living organism's biological response to a stress stimulus. He investigated the organism's success and failure in the biological adaptation to stress. Selye's model of stress adaptation is characterized by three stages: the alarm-reaction stage, the resistance stage, and the exhaustion stage. Stimuli for stress in the alarm stage (ie. physical training, illness, injury, shock, emotional difficulties etc.) causes corresponding physiological reactions to evolve. Sympathetic nervous stimulation is increased producing elevated levels of circulating cortisol. Catecholamines (adrenaline and noradrenaline) are also elevated in the alarm stage. These functions are necessary to produce the 'flight or fight' response in the organism. Selye (1956) observed that with prolonged periods of exposure to stress, the adrenal cortex becomes enlarged, and ulceration may occur in the stomach due to increases in sympathetic innervation, and atrophy of the lymphatic system may result. The resistance or adaptation stage follows this initial stage of arousal. The organism must be able to reduce the effects of the stressor to a manageable level, and thus be able to meet requirements of the stressful situation. Selye (1956) identified this defense mechanism as a decrease in corticoid activity in order to promote adaptation, although if the corticoid activity remains elevated, other functions may be compromised. In other words, the 'fight or flight' response necessary for immediate survival takes precedence over secondary lines of defense such as inflammation or reproduction. In the final stage, exhaustion, the organism is unable to adequately adapt to the stressors. Selye (1956) suggested there is an inability to defend against other external agents, in that adaptive agents may be depleted while the corticoids are elevated. Selye (1956) recognized the importance of establishing an adequate stressor to promote physiological adaptations, however, with prolonged training, the stressor must be imposed over a long period of time. The athlete may be susceptible to evolving into the 'exhaustion stage', and must take proactive steps to avoid reaching this state.

The Methodology of Prolonged Training and Overtraining

Identification of the overtraining state involves a multifaceted approach, which requires an examination of change in the individual's physiological, metabolic, psychological and performance states over a period of time. Lehmann, Foster and Keul (1993) defined overtraining syndrome as the accumulation of fatigue (both exercise and non-exercise), reductions in physical performance, alterations in mood states, presence of muscular stiffness/soreness and a decline in competitive competence over a period of weeks and months. Mackinnon and Hooper (1991) suggested that a 5 to 15% decline in competition performance is not uncommon in overtrained athletes. By far, the most noticeable and overt indicators of overtraining are prolonged fatigue (lasting longer than 1 week), performance decrements, and alterations in mood states (Mackinnon and Hooper, 1991).

Overtrained states have been observed to exist in one of two forms, each of which is a function of the type of exercise that is used in training. Sympathetic overtraining is characterized by an increase in sympathetic innervation at rest, which produces alterations in physiologic functioning such as increased resting heart rate, blood pressure, and weight loss, insomnia and emotional liability. Furthermore, it has been suggested that sympathetic overtraining is more closely associated with explosive, non-endurance anaerobic type physical activity (Kuipers and Keizer, 1988; Vos et al, 1992). Thus the judo athlete is more likely to be susceptible to sympathetic overtraining. In contrast, parasympathetic overtraining is characterized by sympathetic inhibition and parasympathetic dominance, and may be diagnosed after a considerable length of time. Parasympathetic overtraining may be an advanced state of overtraining that is associated with exhaustion of the neuro-endocrine system. Endurance athletes have been shown to be more susceptible to experiencing this form (parasympathetic) of overtraining, which is characterized by early fatigue, low resting pulse rate, higher levels of sleep than normal, and poor endurance performance (Kuipers and Keizer, 1988; Vos et al, 1992). If not corrected, long-term changes in catecholamine, hematological and endocrine levels will occur. At this stage, recovery is a lengthy process, which may require several weeks to months off from training.

Overtraining in Judo Athletes: A Case Study

Overtraining occurs when overloading and stress exceeds recovery and adaptation. In order for overtraining to truly take place, there must be an adequate period of recovery from training stress. If recovery is not restored within 1 to 2 weeks of rest, then overtraining may in fact have occurred (Vos et al, 1992). Overtraining can be identified by specific physiological and psychological symptoms. Subjects who then demonstrate these responses may be in or are fast approaching a state of overtraining. Overtraining in anaerobic based sports (explosive, non-endurance based activity) demonstrate alterations in sympathetic functioning, producing symptoms such as increased resting heart rate and blood pressure, weight loss, insomnia and emotional liability (Vos et al, 1992).

A study by Callister et al (1990) investigated the effects of training on elite U.S. judo athletes after 4 weeks of regular training, and 6 weeks of induced overtraining. Performance evaluations for strength, aerobic and anaerobic power were made via both lab and field tests. Resting heart rate, blood pressure, body weight, percent body fat, and changes in oxygen uptake were monitored to determine if an overtrained state did occur. Vos et al (1992) reports that high intensity sessions applied over a short duration is most beneficial for inducing overtraining. The sparing sessions (randori) consisted of 3 minute matches with a rest interval of approximately 30 seconds

Overtraining can lead to poor performance results.

between each match. Practice sessions typically lasted 2 to 2.5 hours a day. Furthermore, resistance weight training was performed 2–3 times per week, mainly during the morning hours. Results indicated that only strength decreased significantly throughout the introduction of high volume training, and that levels of VO_2 max, heart rate and body weight did not change, and as a result, it is questionable whether or not a true state of overtraining took place. At the conclusion of the study, there was no indication of a recovery period in order to determine if subjects were not able to return to baseline levels. Sources have suggested that overtraining can not take place if athletes return to normal levels within a set time period of approximately 2 to 3 weeks (Vos et al, 1992). The present study did, however, sufficiently represent the population it intended too. The author contended that the training regime identified did present an identical format to that of other national team programs. In particular, it identified the heavy load (high volume) of judo specific training immediately prior to major competition events, which is extremely characteristic of judo training regimes. It was concluded that these elite athletes may be in an existing state of overtraining, and that performance gains would be suppressed. Callister et al (1990) also identified that overtraining may occur in absence of the symptomatic physical signs (of both sympathetic and para-sympathetic derivations). Therefore, monitoring elite judo athletes via physiological means may not be the most effective format in identifying overtraining, and in many cases, it may be too late in its conclusion.

The Physiological Effects of Reduced Training and Detraining
Several researchers have suggested that performance decrements are often indicative of fatigue associated with overtraining (Fry et al, 1992; Houmard, 1991; Kuipers and Keizer, 1988; Lehmann, Dickhuth, Gendrisch, Lazar, Kaminski, Aramendi, Peterke, Wieland and Keul, 1991; Shepley, MacDougall, Cipriano, Sutton, Tarnopolsky and Coates, 1992). Some individuals have reported performance improvements with reductions in training loads over a period ranging from 6 to 21 days (Houmard, 1991; Shepley et al, 1992). It has been suggested that athletes who demonstrate overtraining symptoms have a decreased maximal working capacity and plasma lactate levels. This decrease in plasma lactate level may be explained by the decrease in sympathetic activation during exercise (Kuipers and Keizer, 1988). Physiological changes with detraining and reduced training have been reported to occur within days or weeks after the cessation of training, and results in a loss of both sub-maximal and maximal performance (VO_2) of 25% following 15 days of inactivity. Furthermore, it has also been reported to result in an 8% decrease in time to fatigue following 2 to 4 weeks of detraining (Neufer, 1989). It has been suggested that significant reductions in VO_2 occur within 10 to 21 days following the cessation of training. Specifically, reductions in VO_2 following 21 days of bed rest contributed to a 17–28% decrease in performance (Neufer, 1989). Evidence exists which supports the decrease in VO_2 to reductions in cardiac output and a-vO_2 (arterial-venous) differences (Astrand and Rodahl, 1986). The reduction in VO_2 during the early stages of detraining (2 to 4 weeks) has been reported to occur as a result of lower stoke volumes, which may in turn cause an increase in maximal heart rate, however, further decreases in VO_2 are

largely due to a decline in a-vO_2 difference. Blood volume has also been shown to change with declines in plasma volume, primarily due to a loss in intravascular protein content (Neufer, 1989).

In a review by Neufer (1989), it was reported that as much as 3.5% in total hemoglobin can be lost following 2 to 4 weeks of detraining, and may explain the overall 6% decrease in VO_2 associated with detraining. Overall, lower plasma volumes can severely limit cardiac filling, which may reduce the mechanics of blood transport. Detraining can also effect pre-load and after-load myocardial contractility during both rest and exercise conditions. This may explain a lower stroke volume and consequently lower cardiac output, in so far as lower pre-load levels are associated with reductions in cardiac hypertrophy (Neufer, 1989). Skeletal muscle oxidative enzyme concentration has been reported to decrease following detraining, however, they are more causally linked with changes in sub-maximal exercise. An investigation by Coyle et al (1985) as reported by Neufer (1989) indicated that a 40% decrease in mitochondrial enzyme activity and a 21% increase in LDH (lactate dehydrogenase) activity were found following 8 weeks of detraining. Changes in capillarization and blood flow have also been observed following inactivity, however, they may not depreciate as quickly as other parameters. Neufer (1989) suggested that reductions in capillary density also reduce muscle blood flow, thus limiting the overall availability of oxygen to the muscle and can contribute to reductions in performance.

The Effects of Reduced Training on Performance
Houmard (1991) studied performance following a reduction of training volumes in collegiate runners. Training frequency was reduced by 50% for a 10 day period (a 70% to 80% reduction in training volume). The results of the study indicated that maximal heart rate and VO_2 were not altered with reduced training (66.8 ml.kg.$^{-1}$min^{-1} versus 66.0 ml.kg.$^{-1}$min^{-1} for normal and reduced training, respectively). Several studies, as cited by Houmard (1991), revealed that measurements in VO_2, maximal heart rate, and maximal speed or workload in elite distance runners were not diminished with reductions of 70% to 80% training volume for 10 to 28 days. Furthermore, Houmard (1991) reported that muscle power performance will be maintained and even improved following a 6 to 14 day taper with sufficient training frequency and intensity.

A study by Shepley et al, (1992) examined the physiological effects of a 7 day taper in middle distance runners following 8 weeks of training. Three tapers were used; a high intensity/low volume taper (HIT), a low intensity/high volume taper (LIT), and a rest only taper (ROT). The results of the investigation indicated that maximal oxygen consumption was unaffected in all three tapers, and strength increased significantly in all three tapers. Total blood volume, red cell volume and citrate synthetase activity increased significantly with the HIT. Shepley et al (1992) concluded that performance improvements can take place in highly trained individuals when intensity is maintained, and volume reduced.

Many sources reported an improvement in performance with the implementation of a reduced training load following heavy training (Budget, 1990; Fry et al 1991;

Regular blood analysis is an important part of preventing overtraining.

Houmard, 1991; Shepley et al, 1992; Lehmann et al, 1991). Furthermore, several researchers have suggested that overtraining will not occur if athletes return to normal levels within a set time period of approximately 2 to 3 weeks (Fry et al, 1992; Kuipers and Keizer, 1988; Vos et al, 1992). This improvement in performance was shown to be contingent on the variables of training, primarily intensity, duration and frequency. It does appear, however, that with the introduction of a taper, an over-compensation effect takes place, and fatigue is drastically reduced. As a result, use of tapers in elite training programs is both fairly commonplace and effective.

Red and White Blood Cell Responses to Prolonged Training

Prolonged exposure to training has been demonstrated to produce cardiovascular changes that range from increases in resting blood pressure and heart rate, to a slow return of post-exercise heart rate to normal (Newhouse, 1984; Vos et al, 1992). Symptoms of overtraining have been associated with a decrease in the hemoglobin concentration and hematocrit due to anemia and/or hemolysis (Houmard, 1991). Budget, (1990) has differentiated between true anemia (iron deficiency), and low hemoglobin levels due to increases in plasma volume as a response to training. Serum ferritin concentrations are sensitive to high volume training loads in judo athletes (Malczewska et al, 2000). It has been observed that serum ferritin levels as low as 12 µg/L can be tolerated without any effect on performance (Budget, 1990).

A study by Fry et al, (1992) examined hematological changes in response to 10 days of intensive interval training (twice per day), followed by 5 days of recovery. Performance decrements occurred at the conclusion of the training, but returned to baseline levels. Blood analysis indicated an elevated expression of lymphocyte antigens after training and recovery, with serum ferritin concentrations being significantly depressed from pre-training to recovery states. This demonstrates that hemoglobin and hematocrit assessments alone may not be very accurate in determining physiological fatigue states of athletes. Most researchers suggested that hematological assessments be used in conjunction with other tests, in order to obtain an effective evaluation of fatigue and adaptations to the training program (Mackinnon and Hooper, 1991; Houmard, 1991; Fry et al, 1992). More commonly, over trained athletes have demonstrated a susceptibility to iron deficiency, and low hemoglobin levels, as opposed to anaerobically trained athletes. Deficiencies may be explained on the basis of depressed bone marrow iron stores from various causes such as low dietary iron intake, sweating, gastrointestinal blood loss during heavy efforts, and increased red blood cell turnover (Vos et al, 1992). Exercise stress has been shown to effect levels of white blood cells within the body. This in turn can affect an individual's immune function and expose them to a greater chance of obtaining an infection. Specifically, there is a marked increase in white blood cell (WBC) counts in relation to the duration of exercise, and consequently, this relationship was more dependent upon intensity than duration of activity (Osterud, Olsen and Wilsgard, 1989). Application to judo performance involves the coach and sport scientist monitoring blood profiles to look for any early indications of fatigue. Typically, this would be a decrease in red blood cell (RBC) and an increase in WBC counts. Often this can occur without any other physical or psychological symptoms, and is therefore considered to be an important precursor in identifying overtrained athletes. When this situation occurs, training volume and intensity need to be reduced to avoid entering into an overtrained state.

Endocrine Responses to Prolonged Training

Prolonged periods of training produce changes in the endocrine system in exercising humans. Exercise stress has both short and long-term influences on the endocrine profiles of the individual. The most overt changes, however, may be seen in the variations in concentrations following exercise stress. The research literature has indicated that variations in serum testosterone, cortisol and catecholamine levels are most common with prolonged training and overtrained athletes. The benefit in monitoring these hormones is in identifying those athletes who are at risk of progressing into an overtrained state.

Catecholamine Concentration

Prolonged periods of stress will promote hypothalamic dysfunction. The hypothalamus co-ordinates endocrine, behavioral and autonomic nervous system functions. Stress activates the hypothalamus, which in turn influences an increase in the adrenocorticotrophic hormone (ACTH) releasing factor. This increase activates the anterior pituitary, which releases ACTH to activate the adrenal cortex. An increase in neuroendocrine innervation causes activation of the pituitary adreno-cortical system. The result is large increases in circulating plasma levels of catecholamines and cortisol

(Kuipers and Keizer, 1988; Newhouse, 1984). Several changes in metabolic function have been associated with overtrained states. Catecholamines have been shown to increase during exercise due to a release of noradrenaline from sympathetic nerve endings, and provide the means whereby an increase in heart rate, stroke volume, basal metabolic rate and ventilation can result (Boone, Sherraden, Pierzchala, Berger and VanLoon, 1992; Gaesser, 1994; Kuipers and Keizer, 1988). Furthermore, this can result in an overall increase in blood shunting due to the vasoconstriction and vasodilation of tissues in response to the increase in catecholamines (Newhouse, 1984). Following prolonged exercise, plasma catecholamine levels have been observed to fall well below initial levels due to a suppressed catecholamines response. Thus it is this stress response that allows catecholamine to be employed as a reliable indicator of stress. (Kuipers and Keizer, 1988).

Some researchers have indicated that overtraining may be associated with suppressed catecholamine levels, and may serve as one factor to be examined in the monitoring of overtraining. Furthermore, nocturnal catecholamine excretion levels are a strong indicator of intrinsic sympathetic activity (Mackinnon and Hooper, 1991). A study by Lehmann et al, (1991) examined catecholamine excretion levels of middle and long distance runners after periods of high volume endurance training. The runners demonstrated lower levels of catecholamine excretion than baseline after four weeks of overload training. In addition to this, runners were also monitored on a four point complaint index, which demonstrated a relationship between statements of fatigue and excretion levels of catecholamine. Lehmann et al (1991), concluded that a decrease in catecholamine levels may indicate a sign of overexertion, as observed in endurance based (parasympathetic overtraining) events.

Testosterone Concentration
Prolonged training has been shown to increase the concentration of both serum testosterone and cortisol. Furthermore, it has been observed that during periods of intensive stress lasting several days, serum testosterone falls and serum cortisol increases in trained athletes (Hakkinen, Keskinen, Alen, Komi and Kauhanen, 1989). A study by Hackney (1989) examined testosterone responses in endurance trained males. Normal resting blood testosterone levels in adult males ranged from 3.0 to 11.0 µg/L, the majority of which was produced by the Leydig cells of the testes. Testosterone serves both reproductive and anabolic roles, and regulation is performed via a negative feedback involving the hypothalamic-pituitary-testicular axis. The majority (97%) of circulating testosterone is transported bound to carrier proteins. The remaining 3% is unbound and circulates as 'free testosterone'. 'Free' testosterone is considered the biologically active form, and the combination of both bound and free testosterone are referred to as total testosterone (Hackney, 1989).

Research has shown that the effects of prolonged training on testosterone levels have revealed that trained athletes tend to display lower resting levels of testosterone. Investigators have reported that low levels of free testosterone are characteristic of overtrained individuals (Lehmann, Foster and Keul, 1993; Fry et al, 1992). This is often a function of production, secretion and metabolic clearance. Average testos-

Regular physiological testing and monitoring of the athlete significantly increases the chances of experiencing peak performance.

terone production in adult males have been determined to be 7000 µg/day. Metabolic clearance of testosterone have been estimated at 1100 µg/day, which is a result of both target tissue uptake and hepatic degradation (Hackney, 1989). Testosterone responses to short term, maximal exercise produced an increase in circulating levels, which may be a result of hemo-concentration, reduced clearance and/or a response in elevated catecholamine (Hackney, 1989). The responses to sub-maximal exercise were somewhat varied, with reports ranging from little or no increases, to even decreases in concentration.

It has been well established that decreased testosterone production in sub-maximal exercise may be as a result of reduced testicular blood flow during exercise, therefore compromising hepatic blood flow and metabolic clearance (Hackney, 1989). Studies which have reported low levels of circulating testosterone were those which examined highly trained subjects who had been training for a minimum of 5 years, and were competitive at elite levels. Therefore, these results may reflect the long-term effects of training. Although it has been well established that testosterone production and clearance is sensitive to prolonged training, there is little evidence that demonstrates prolonged training produces significant effects on testosterone dependent functions in the body. It is evident that extremely high or low levels of testosterone over an extended period of time is associated with certain conditions (ie. overtraining), and that monitoring testosterone profiles may be of value in assessing training adaptations.

Hakkinen et al (1989) investigated serum hormone concentrations during prolonged training in both strength and endurance trained athletes. It is known that exercise intensity and duration promote acute responses in the endocrine system. The corresponding changes in the endocrine system to endurance training primarily involve adaptations in energy production through oxidative metabolism. Hakkinen et al (1989) measured weight lifters and swimmers at four month intervals during the course of one year. The study results demonstrated that during the most intensive part of the training year, small but insignificant changes of serum testosterone, free testosterone and cortisol did occur in both groups. These results indicated that mean serum cortisol for the endurance trained group significantly increased during the year. It was concluded that testosterone and cortisol levels do fluctuate and are sensitive to training loads throughout the year. Therefore, hormonal profiles may then prove effective in the monitoring of exercise stress and prevent conditions of overtraining.

Fry, Morton, Garcia-Webb and Keast (1991) examined endocrine responses in 14 subjects of varying fitness levels to 2, 4, 8, and 24 hours post-exercise anaerobic interval training. Uric acid, urea, and CPK (creatine phosphokinase) were found to be elevated higher than-pre-exercise levels even after 24 hours post-exercise. Some sources indicate that female judo athletes in particular may even be more sensitive to CPK, LDH and uric acid changes in response to judo training (De Cree et al, 1995). Lactate, CPK, testosterone and cortisol concentrations were elevated by 2 hours post-exercise and returned to normal at 24 hours post-exercise. Testosterone levels, in contrast, eventually fell even lower than pre-exercise levels in recovery. Budget (1990) reinforced this observation by indicating that intense and prolonged exercise will increase cortisol, but decrease levels of testosterone. As a result, the testosterone/cortisol ratio may fall in response to prolonged periods of training. Kuipers and Keizer (1988) suggested that low testosterone levels following exercise might be the result of an inhibition of testicular secretion, due to an increase in luteinizing hormone. In conclusion, Fry et al (1992) observed that hormonal imbalances due to intensive training were not totally reversed within a 24 hour period. Although this study did present a sound hormonal profile as a result of intensive exercise, it may not be directly applicable to overtraining in elite athletes. These (elite) individuals have been subjected to a high volume and intensity of training for a prolonged period, unlike that of the varying fitness levels of the subjects in the aforementioned study. Consequently, the degree of response would vary as a consequence of the higher levels of fitness. These studies do then illustrate the varied response of testosterone to physical activity.

Cortisol Concentration

The monitoring of cortisol levels has been reported to be an effective way in assessing stress (Sapse, 1984). It has been documented that stressful situations increase levels of plasma cortisol. Cortisol is divided into 80% corticosteroid binding globin (CBG), 10% serum albumin, and 10% 'free' cortisol (Sapse, 1984). Furthermore, Sapse (1984) has reported that a normal resting level of adult total cortisol has been measured at 12 µg/dl, with large increases in total cortisol after surgery (24–48 µg/dl) and infection (63–99 µg/dl). Increments in plasma cortisol have been found after exercise, however it appears that cortisol returns to pre-exercise levels after cessation of exercise (Kuipers and Keizer, 1988). It has been observed that following long lasting intense exercise, cortisol and catecholamine levels may decrease below normal levels for several days due to decreased catecholamine synthesis. Kuipers and Keizer (1988) have suggested that this decrease in catecholamine and cortisol levels results in a decrease in mobilization of the energy reserve, which consequently lowers physical work capacity. A decrease in work capacity may predispose the athlete to injury.

A study by Tsai, Johansson, Pousette, Tegelman, Carlstrom and Hemmingsson (1991) examined the effects of cortisol and androgen concentrations in elite endurance athletes. Nine elite orienteers and seven cross-country skiers were assessed in the off-season, pre-season and competitive season to determine relative changes in hormonal concentrations throughout one season. Venous blood samples were taken during nocturnal fasting procedures the following morning. Cortisol values increased significantly from the off to the competitive season, and female mean concentrations were higher than that of males during the competitive season. Although there was no difference between the skiers or the orienteers, there was a difference in levels of concentration between gender. Furthermore, it was suggested that the ratio of free testosterone to cortisol may be effective in the early detection of overtraining. As a result, Tsai et al (1991) stated that female endurance athletes adapt differently than male endurance athletes to training. Consequently, female cortisol responses may be more sensitive to increases in training load than males. The endocrine system is highly sensitive to the physiological demands of exercise. The most important hormonal changes are increases in both catecholamine and cortisol. Unlike testosterone, these usually return to baseline levels with adequate rest. Monitoring these hormones throughout the training year provides an effective means in preventing overtraining.

Summary

As we can see, overtrained states are a complex and long term application. Prevention is in the early detection and predication of those athletes who may be exposed. Detection is done via multiple examinations of blood, performance and psychological parameters. The key application for the judo athlete and coach is to be aware of the increased risk of developing an overtrained state when performing both high intensity training/competition with repeated weight loss. In fact, most serious and dehabilitating injuries occur during training camps; a period where both volume and training intensity are typically at a maximum. The solution to this dilemma is relatively simple. Adequate rest, hydration, recovery from competition/training and regular physiological monitoring.

PART THREE
PSYCHO-BEHAVIOURAL FACTORS
IN JUDO PERFORMANCE

In all aspects of sport from novice to world class, there is an aspect of mental preparation. Often the best example of this is the television sport celebrity who commonly attributes a successful competition event to a 'mental victory'. World calibre performance is most often due to excellent mental skills. These are skills learned from trial and error throughout a competitive career. More advanced training programs learn to incorporate aspects of mental preparation within training programs to more accurately imitate what the athlete is most likely to encounter in the competition arena. It is known that internal physiological and biochemical parameters influence the behaviour and mood of humans. Psychological demeanor is an indication of physical status, in so far as if the body is healthy, the mind will be happy. Overtrained states are highly predicable when monitoring these situations closely. Section three will examine two components of psycho-behavioural aspects of sport performance applied to judo. First, is to examine common psycho-behavioural characteristics of elite athletes. Second, is to identify psychological markers of overtraining. By taking this approach, the coach or sport scientist will have an understanding of what psycho-behavioural traits to strive for in order to re-produce for both training and competition, and which traits to avoid or monitor as possible indicators of overtraining.

Successful vs. Unsuccessful Athletes
Competitive athletes tend to demonstrate similar attributes in both their preparation for competition, as well as their attitudes during competition (Garfield, 1984; Martens, 1988). Although most elite athletes admit to mental preparation as a crucial element to their success, mental training often tends to be neglected or superficially included with training programs. Coaches and trainers often lack the techniques or proper education with the introduction of mental training, and therefore it is often ignored when producing the yearly training plan. The majority of successful athletes have used some form of mental preparation prior to their best ever performances. Most successful athletes experience a higher dream frequency, tend to self verbalize more often, use mental imagery, and have pre-determined methods of coping for stress (Heyman, 1982). Furthermore, successful athletes tended to be more self confi-

dent, in addition to imagining themselves participating in successful performances more often (Heyman, 1982).

A study by Gould et al (1981) done on characteristics of successful and non-successful wrestlers, examined the athlete's cognitive states and their respective performance in competition. An 11 point Lickert scale questionnaire was completed prior to a major competitive event to determine their competitive mental states. They were rated on i) anxiety/coping responses, ii) pre-match mental preparation and self-talk, iii) best and worst performances. Results indicated that successful wrestlers stated that they were closer to reaching their maximum competitive potential, and that they were more confident of success than those wrestlers who were not as overt about their potential. It was found that 95% of successful medal placers and 97% of non-successful medal placers were correctly placed. Another study by Highlen and Bennett (1983) rated amateur wrestlers on confidence levels during wrestling qualifiers. They found that wrestling qualifiers were rated higher on self-confidence and had fewer negative thoughts prior to competition than non-qualifiers. The study also found that the use of imagery and self-talk differentiated between successful and non-successful divers. In general, successful athletes view themselves with high self esteem, self-confidence and possess effective competitive coping skills. They also tended to score lower on anxiety levels in both pre-competitive and competitive states. Finally, they used some form of mental preparation prior to and/or during competition.

Psychological Traits of Olympic Athletes

World and Olympic class athletes demonstrate some interesting patterns of behaviour. Orlick and Partington (1988) interviewed 235 Canadian Olympic athletes who participated in the 1984 winter and summer Olympics. The following is a brief summary of what were common elements of success and those factors that interfered with performance:

COMMON ELEMENTS OF SUCCESS

> quality training sessions
> use of clear daily goals throughout training
> imagery training
> use of simulation training
> mental preparation for competition (4 stages identified)
> learned elements of success
> performance blocks at the games (3 identified)

Almost all (99%) of these Olympic athletes used some form of mental preparation. It is a skill that is learned through competitive experience and practice. Orlick and Partington (1988) specified the following idealistic traits which were present in Olympic athletes: (a) total commitment in pursuit of excellence (b) quality training sessions (c) well established competition plan. Attentional focus and quality of performance imagery were directly related to performance at the games. Performance blocks were (a) changing patterns of training (b) late selection to the team, and (c) an inability to refocus from distractions. Orlick and Partington (1988) concluded that many athletes might have performed better if they were better prepared for coping with the many distractions at the games.

Characteristics of Peak Performance

Ideal sport performances seem to have some interesting similarities. Cohn (1991) studied psychological traits in elite golfers (PGA) and categorized identical characteristics in peak performance. The interview consisted of open-ended questions based on repeated statements throughout the session. Cohn found these qualities of peak performance reported at least 80% of the time:

PEAK PERFORMANCE QUALITIES

> movements that are automatic and effortless
> immersed in the present
> feeling of control
> ability to remain relaxed
> fun and enjoyment
> an absence of fear
> high levels of self confidence

Rehearsing past successes is an important part of preparing for peak performance.

Cohn's results were similar to other's (Garfield, 1984) in identifying characteristics of peak performance states. Garfield presents a mental training program, which requires the athlete to systematically prepare by reliving their best ever performance experiences through visualization. He incorporates several exercises for relaxation, confidence and anxiety management. It appears that peak performance states experienced by elite athletes are by enlarge transient, physical and psychological states of superior functioning. In many cases, authorities attempt to bring about this state by trying to reproduce the above stated qualities. The contribution of the preceding information illustrates the importance in the development of confidence and competitive experience in elite athletes. Furthermore, athletes must be able to utilize tactics and strategies to manage competitive anxiety and stress when preparing for competition. Regular mental preparation, which is integrated within the practice session, appears to be an effective means in facilitating optimum performance.

Psychological & Behavioural Responses to Prolonged Training & Overtraining

Various sources have identified changes in mood state, behavior, motivation to train, irritability, depression, insomnia, loss of libido, and loss of appetite as signs of overreaching and overtraining (Budget, 1990; Fry et al, 1992; Hooper, Mackinnon, Howard, Gordon and Bachmann, 1995; Morgan, Brown, Raglin, O'Connor and Ellickson, 1987; Sapse, 1984; Vos et al, 1992). Hormonal changes induced by prolonged training cause a variety of behavioral responses. Increased catecholamine and cortisol effect the central nervous system, which may cause anxiety and depression to occur (Sapse, 1984). It is known that hormonal levels can influence behaviour and can even be linked to aggressive and even competitive behaviour (Salvadora et al, 1999). The following examines states of fatigue, alterations in mood states and susceptibility to injury in illness as it relates to training and overtraining.

The Relationship of Fatigue to Lactate

Some researchers have demonstrated the existence of a relationship between participation in intense exercise and self reports of fatigue and exertion. A study by Synder, Jeukendrup, Hesselink, Kuipers and Foster (1992), examined well trained cyclists over 6 weeks of training in normal, overtrained and recovery states. Blood lactate (HLac) analysis was made and compared to Borg's Rating of Perceived Exertion (RPE) scale in regular testing every 2 weeks. The results of the study demonstrated that the HLac:RPE ratio decreased throughout the overtrained period (29% in week 3, and 48% in week 4). Lactate concentration decreased with training, however, RPE values were maintained. Synder et al (1992), suggested that the decline in the ratio was due to an overall decrease in the utilization of glycogen, although another possible explanation was the improvement in lactate clearance rates. In the recovery state, the HLac:RPE ratio was found to return to normal. This study provided evidence that perceived fatigue can serve as a good indicator of overreached states.

Alterations in Mood States

The most highly recognized work in the monitoring of mood states has been done by Morgan et al (1987), who examined mood states of varsity swimmers throughout a typical year with high volume training performed during the competitive season. This investigation utilized the Profile of Mood States (POMS), which is a questionnaire composed of 65 items measuring various emotions. A complete score is determined by adding five negative mood states (tension, depression, anger, fatigue, and confusion), and subtracting the one positive mood state (vigor). Elite athletes and active individuals tend to score lower than the population average on the five negative mood states, and score higher than average on the one positive mood state (Morgan et al, 1987). Several studies were performed on the same population demonstrating a general mood disturbance in the mid-season, which included peak training. These changes in mood were due to an increase in fatigue and a decrease in vigor. In summary, Morgan et al (1987) indicated that alterations in fatigue and vigor generally precede more serious mood disturbances (depression or anxiety). The POMS also demonstrated an increase in anger and depression. Depression also seems to be related to overtraining, as previously cited, however, it is worthwhile to report that mood states did improve after titration of the training load.

Mental focus is an integral part of peak performance.

A study by Hooper, Mackinnon, Gordon and Bachmann (1993) investigated hormonal changes throughout a 6 month training season in elite swimmers, leading up to peak performance for the World team trials. The aim of the project was to monitor signs and symptoms of overtraining throughout the season via hormonal and mood state changes. The athletes were evaluated via a self-reported training log and POMS (profile of mood states) questionnaires. Blood samples were collected at early (2–3 weeks), mid (12–14 weeks), late seasons (5–6 weeks), a taper period (3–5 days) and post competition (1–3 days). The results demonstrated that 3 of the 14 swimmers exhibited signs of overtraining, and that these three were female athletes. Moreover, fatigue ratings were higher in mid-season, tapering and post-competition periods. Cortisol and epinephrine levels throughout the whole season were not significantly different between the stale and well-trained swimmers. Norepinephrine levels, however, were found to be greater for the stale compared to the well-trained swimmers during the taper period. Hooper et al (1993) reported that the stale swimmers had actually maintained a higher volume of training than the well-trained swimmers. This was most likely due to their poor performance through the season, which motivated them to work harder in an attempt to improve performance. In conclusion, Hooper et al (1993) reported significant findings in the incidence of negative mood states with corresponding increases in training load. As well, Morgan et al (1987) also observed that these negative mood states disappeared with tapering and unloading of training volume. The changes in mood state were directly related to the corresponding changes in other physiological parameters (endocrine, cardiovascular etc.). Morgan et al (1987) concluded that use of the POMS provides a effective means for evaluating individual training loads. In summary, ratings of fatigue and mood states may be associated with increases in training loads. The previous studies have illustrated that monitoring of training stress via psychological and behavioral changes are related to the corresponding physiological changes. Regular use of such measurements may enable the coach to assess training progression, and then implement the appropriate load changes.

Susceptibility to Illness and Injury

Several authorities have indicated that the increase in the occurrence and incidence of injuries is both a sign and result of overtraining (Budget, 1990; Callister, Callister, Fleck and Dudley, 1990; Fry et al, 1992; Kibler, Chandler and Stracener, 1992). Physical activity places demands on the musculoskeletal system, which may result in mechanical trauma or injuries. Kibler et al (1992) suggested that injuries due to overtraining may range from sub-clinical (as seen in decrements in performance), to overt (an injury which inhibits performance). Newhouse (1984) also identified overuse injuries (ie. tendonitis, or mechanical musculoskeletal) as a possible outcome of overtraining. The mechanisms responsible for this situation appears to be due to the large amounts of circulating cortisone. Cortisol acts as an anti-inflammatory and inhibits growth, therefore protein synthesis will be compromised. Training increases protein catabolism, and recovery promotes protein re-synthesis. Kuipers and Keizer (1988) reported that with incomplete recovery, premature fatigue of the motor unit pool will occur during exercise performance. Therefore, the individual will require an increase in nervous innervation to generate the comparable levels of force. This may place a greater demand on the muscular system than the individual can meet, thus resulting in an injury. In addition, other researchers suggested that the chronically fatigued athlete who has insufficient glycogen levels is more susceptible to injury. The greater energy costs and higher heart rates in fatigued athletes may decrease the economy of movement, and may produce mechanical errors in technique, thus predisposing the individual to injury (Mackinnon and Hooper, 1991).

Other investigators have reported that fatigued and overtrained athletes experience a higher incidence of colds, flues and infections, which take a longer time than usual to recover (Budget, 1990; Fry et al, 1992; Hooper et al, 1995; Newhouse, 1984; Vos et al, 1992). Cortisol has been identified as a powerful immuno-suppressor, thus lowering the immune resistance of the body (Sapse, 1984). It reduces the level of T-helper cells, and suppresses fibroblast growth. T-lymphocytes and fibroblasts are essential for the production of interferon, therefore there may be a causal relation between stress and diminished immune response to viral infections (Sapse, 1984). Selye (1956) demonstrated that during the alarm stage, there is atrophy of the lymphatic system. It is suggested that this may be the result of a diminished number of circulating lymphocytes in the blood, which will impair resistance to viral infections. Budget (1990) confirmed this by reporting that following exercise, there is a release of white blood cells (WBC), causing a temporary leucocytosis. Following intense exercise, Budget (1990) has also observed a reduced T-helper cell:T-suppressor cell ratio, however, this did not correlate with temporary suppression of lymphocyte function. An alternative explanation for diminished immune response may be due to reduced plasma glutamine levels. Budget (1990) illustrated that plasma glutamine levels provide 35% of the necessary energy for lymphocyte metabolism, therefore if lymphocyte metabolism is inhibited, this may account for the immuno-suppression response. In either case, the exact explanation for the reduction in immune function is not exactly known, however, it appears that prolonged exposure to exercise training without an adequate recovery period produces specific responses in the endocrine system. These changes influence the contribution of the lymphocytes and T-cells, which in turn alter their effectiveness in deterring the onset of infection or illness.

We can see an inverse relationship between peak performance and fatigued or overtrained states. Specifically, psyco-behavioural symptoms of overtraining often precede more devastating physiological changes. The judo coach and athlete need to use behavioural inventories throughout the training year to screen for symptoms of overtraining. Early detection and proper rest and recovery will minimize the probability of injuries and infections, allowing the athlete to focus on effective training.

PART FOUR
PLANNING THE TRAINING SESSION AND TRAINING YEAR

Following a review of the physiology and psychology of judo athletes, the coach must be able to systematically plan and prepare a satisfactory training plan aimed at maximizing the physiological changes desired for competition performance. Training programs and sessions must be designed and implemented to have an increasing grade of challenge (load and volume of training stimulus) in order to adequately prepare the athlete for subsequent training and competitions. Early on in the athlete's career, training focus is generally designed for preparing the individual physically in order that they can accommodate the stress of prolonged training. In other words, fundamentals are emphasized (aerobic conditioning and absolute strength) and are the easiest to train and monitor initially. As the athlete physically and psychologically matures, the level of competition increases. Consequently, the athlete must adjust training to reflect the tactical and strategic demands of competition, rather than focus on physical preparation. This is best exemplified in the behaviour of senior athletes and those individuals who are able to return to high level competition (ie. 2–3 Olympic Games) over and over again. Physically, they are at a level to be competitive, but eventually surpass their opponents and win both matches and competitions due to a greater level of experience and skill. The following section will examine the design and implementation of the judo training session. First, will be a brief review of nutrition and weight loss for the judo athlete for both training and competition. Second, will be a review of the energy systems required for judo and some examples of how to structure a judo training session to incorporate these principles. Finally, will be an examination of both a strength and mental training program for the complete training year. All previous sections will be covered in detail in the sample annual training plan.

Nutrition and Weight Loss for Judo Performance
Any part of a solid training program involves dietary modifications for both optimal performance and for weight loss. The type, quantity and combinations of nutritional selections must be able to meet the demand of the athlete. The recommended daily nutritional intake presented by Canada's Food Guide suggests a daily ingestion of

nutrients based on portions or servings. Eating for sport performance is often nothing more than just eating smart and making healthy choices. The concern should be is the judo athlete eating enough, and what and how to eat when losing weight? The focus of this section is to provide a very basic introduction into nutrition, with an emphasis on how to safely and effectively lose weight for competition. More detailed information can be found in any nutrition book, and the reader should consult those references for a more detailed understanding of sports nutrition. All the material presented in the nutrition section has been taken from Whitney et al (1990).

› Milk and Milk Products: 2–3 servings a day
› Meat and Meat Alternatives: 2–3 servings a day
› Fruits and Vegetables: 5–10 servings a day
› Breads and Cereals: 6–11 servings a day
› Fats and Oils: use sparingly; best with mono/polyunsaturated fats

Carbohydrates

This food group is a group or series of sugar chains. Included in this group are sugar chains from fructose (fruit), sucrose, lactose and galactose. Several groups of these sugar chains form glycogen, which are large, complex sugar groups stored in both muscle and liver. Some examples of carbohydrates are from the bread and cereals food groups; pasta, rice and fruits. These sources are the primary choice for exercising muscle. Ideally, 60% of the athlete's diet should be from carbohydrate sources. Manipulation of carbohydrate consumption can influence sport performance. Carbohydrate loading, is a process where the athlete starves the diet of carbohydrates for a period of 3–5 days, and then super-compensates by consuming the majority of the diet with carbohydrates for 3 days. The net effect is both the muscle and liver increase carbohydrate stores above normal levels. The benefit of this strategy is mainly for endurance athletes due to depletion in carbohydrate stores during prolonged exercise. This, however, is not advisable for judo athletes due to the large amounts of water needed to store the glycogen. Thus increasing water retention and body weight, which would impact on the weight loss process.

Proteins

This food group is a series or group of several amino acids together. They form long lists of chains, which are used daily in the production of muscle, hormones and blood. Protein food sources exist in animal sources (dairy, beef, poultry, pork, fish); and non-animal sources (nuts, legumes and soy). The estimated recommended daily nutrient intake of protein is based on the individual's body weight (kilograms) multiplied by a factor of 0.8 to get a determination of the daily amount. Evaluation of an individual's protein need is often done via a nitrogen balance, which measures the amount of nitrogen ingested and excreted in the human body. Excess nitrogen can put an added strain on the excretory system, particularly the kidneys. Some side effects of excess protein may be the production of kidney stones, and as a result, athletes should be careful when supplementing their diet with extra protein (ie. Creatine).

Fats, Vitamins and Minerals

This food group exists in both animal and non-animal sources. These are either saturated fats (animal products), monounsaturated (nuts and olive oils) or polyunsaturated fats (vegetable sources). Fats are an important food source in the healthy diet and are necessary for the production of hormones and body maintenance functions.

Both of these nutrients are necessary for a variety of biological and physiological function. Vitamins are needed for activities such as energy production and tissue growth, whereas minerals are needed for structural components (ie. cells, hormones, teeth, bones). It is imperative to have a daily intake of the essential nutrients, which exist in one of two forms: water soluble vitamins (B complex and C) or fat soluble vitamins (A, D, E and K). Dietary supplementation is only effective if the diet is deficient, or during repeated bouts of weight loss.

The Ideal Athlete Diet

Generally, the ideal diet should involve following the four food groups. Eating a variety of food sources with a variety of colour is an effective guideline. An approximate breakdown should consist of a majority of carbohydrates in the diet. Regular consumption of a minimum of 8 glasses of water daily, however, more is necessary if the person is physically active and/or dehydrated.

IDEAL DIETS ARE:

> 10% saturated fat, 20% unsaturated fat (mono/polyunsaturated fats)
> 12% protein, 48%carbohydrate, 10% sugars
> consists of a variety of foods (lots of colour)
> consume 8 glasses of water daily (double with training)
> substitute refined sugar for fruit sugar
> limit salt and alcohol
> dietary supplement with hard weight loss
> include high fibre foods
> monitor diet with training

Monitoring the Athletic Diet:

Any diet should be monitored on a regular basis to ensure that it is meeting the individual's nutritional requirements. Monitoring strategies included determining the athlete's estimated percent body fat before and during the training season. Variations in the percent body fat throughout the season will reflect physical changes as a result of training. In monitoring an individual's diet, several tools are available for the coach. A simple athlete journal of what food items and relative serving sizes summarizing the total daily caloric intake is very effective. This is important in determining what amount to lose, and more importantly, where in the diet to modify eating habits. A baseline measurement of regular eating habits should be done over the course of 3–5 days, with the servings being expressed as kcal. Every living organism has a set level of calories necessary for maintaining normal healthy bodily function. This amount is determined via calculating their basal metabolic rate (BMR), which provides an estimation of the minimum number of calories necessary to maintain health for a sedentary or non-active person.

CALORIC ANALYSIS

> 1 lbs body fat = 3500 kcal (9 kcal/g)
> BMR/day = 1C x wt (kg) x 24 (ie. 68 x 2 = 1632 kcal)
> judo activity = 5–6 kcal/hr/lbs (6 x 150 = 900 kcal/hr)
> BMR + training = total kcal/day
> intake ≥ output = weight gain
> intake ≤ output = weight loss (diet)

In determining daily caloric consumption, the individual's BMR is added to additional energy costs for training. For example, judo activity during training requires a minimum of 900 to 1200 kcal per hour. This, combined with any additional training sessions (ie. a morning run of 600 kcal per hour) would be summated to produce the caloric score for the day. The focus should be on gradually reducing the total daily caloric intake. Several nutrition resources are available to assist the athlete with monitoring and assessing their individual nutrition patterns, and the reader is encouraged to consult these references for access to these tools.

Effective Weight Loss Strategies
Current IJF regulations require judo competitors to weigh in the day of the event. In so doing, the judo athlete must constantly monitor their body weight and repeatedly be prepared to weigh in, sometimes on a weekly basis. As a result, having an effective weight loss program is very beneficial to judo performance. More than likely, athletes learn how to lose weight for competitions by trial and error and through observation of their peers. Often, mistakes in weight loss are costly both financially and physiologically, and the long-term effects can be problematic. Weight loss practice should be gradually introduced to the judo athlete, and be only involved with those who are both physically and mentally mature.

Weight loss should be done gradually, over a set period of weeks. The duration of the loss corresponds directly with the amount of weight desired to be lost. The athlete should have their individual percent body fat estimated prior and during the training season. Ideally, safe and effective weight loss should not exceed 1–1.5 kg per week. This should be evaluated by morning weight prior to any fluid and/or food consumption. Some effective techniques is to eliminate food consumption following evening training. The athlete should consume their largest meal earlier in the day, and make sure to eat dinner prior to afternoon or evening judo training. If there is no scheduled practice, the athlete should participate in sub-maximal aerobic conditioning for 35–45 minutes followed by stretching. The individual needs to be dressed warm and remain in a heated area following the aerobic activity to maintain elevated body core temperature and metabolism.

EFFECTIVE WEIGHT LOSS

› start early prior to competition
› no more than 2 lbs or 1 kg/week
› eat largest meal in a.m. and no feeding past evening workout (fluids only)
› gradually decrease kcal to 1500/day
› obtain baseline a.m. weight and overnight 'drift weight'
› do not cut fluid intakes until very last 12 hours
› use ice cubes & candies (ie. M&M's) to curb appetites for pre-night weigh in

In addition, the athlete needs to measure baseline body weight prior to and immediately following bed rest. In so doing, they can establish an evening 'drift weight', which is the amount of weight lost overnight while sleeping. Drift weight usually ranges from 0.4–1.3 kg, depending on the weight of the individual. Of course, the heavier the individual, the more weight lost overnight. The purpose in determining a drift weight is to know what weight the athlete has to be at upon going to bed. For example, if the athlete has to be –66.0 kg and has a drift weight of 0.6 kg, then he is to weigh in the night before at 66.6 kg. Several factors can affect drift weight. The harder the weight loss (in other words, losing a greater amount than usual in a shorter period of time), the less effect on the drift weight. If the athlete is de-hydrated and has lost a large amount of water, this too will negatively effect the drift weight. The goal of the night before weigh in is to make the weight division plus the drift weight amount (ie. 66.0 kg + 0.6 kg). It is only at this point that de-hydration be used to make weight. Ideally, the athlete should be a maximum of 1.5–2.0 kg over the weight division. This translates into a day before weight loss of 1.0–1.5 kg only.

For those athletes losing weight, food items to consume the day prior to the weigh in should not be complex carbohydrates. Pastas and rice are problematic due to the need for increased water needed for metabolism and digestion. Although, smaller or easily digestible carbohydrates (ie. infant cereal, applesauce) would be a sufficient alternative. A typical example would be to increase the amount of physical activity in the final week of the weigh in. Rather than participate in long, exhaustive training, the athlete should perform shorter and more frequent physical activity of a mild intensity. For example, a light run or cycle for 30–45 min of 65–75 % of maximal heart rate in the morning, followed by judo training in the afternoon or evening. In each situation, the athlete should have a track-suit on to promote maximal perspiration. The heat and perspiration is extremely important in elevating metabolism necessary for weight loss. In all cases, the athlete should re-hydrate with fluids following training. Following the afternoon or evening training, no food should be consumed, only fluids, until the next morning. The main meal should be consumed prior to evening training. This format should be repeated on a daily basis on the week of the scheduled weigh in. It is imperative to note that successful weight loss is a product of experience, proper diet, and physical fitness. These traits are best reflected in older more senior athletes who are able to physically and psychologically handle the stress and weight loss.

Periodization and The Annual Judo Training Plan
High performance athletics demands complex planning and preparation. Top performance requires the athlete to reach his or her own individual physical, psychological and technical potential. Co-ordinating such a task is the basic principle behind periodized training. Often, too much emphasis might be placed on one component, while neglecting another. The result is poor preparation, inadequate recovery and a failure to reach athletic performance potential. Bompa (1994) identifies the training year as three essential components of preparatory, competitive and transition phases of training. The main determinant in planning the training year is based on the frequency and importance of the competitions during the training year. Each step in the training year is cumulative, in order to progressively increase the training load. With each increase in a macro-cycle, there is an adequate recovery or unloading period to allow regeneration and recovery. The individual training session is the fundamental building block of the training program. Subsequent collections of the training session accumulate during the week produce a micro-cycle, and the accumulation of weekly micro-cycles produce macro-cycles.

In planning the training year, the coach must include all assets necessary to develop the athlete physically and mentally. Regular testing is essential in ensuring if training goals are being met, and are a requirement of most national programs. Training sessions can be adjusted by increasing one of two factors: intensity or volume. Bompa (1994) presents weekly training sessions with varying peaks, and structures the training session accordingly depending the number of desired peaks. The following will provide a brief review of Bompa's (1994) training phases with an application to judo training for an experienced national level athlete preparing for the world championships. Refer to the figure 'Annual Training Plan' to determine when each phase should be introduced. In each phase, differing parts of the training program are interspersed. Each training component (strength, conditioning, mental preparation, diet and technique) is adjusted for both volume and intensity following each successive phase. It is important to note that all training components (both specific and supplemental) must reflect the energy system required for the sport. The majority of training methodology and periodization principles presented are from Bompa (1994).

The Preparatory Phase
The objective of this phase is to develop the general framework for physical, technical, tactical and psychological preparation for the competition phase. It is character-

istic of higher volume training (70% to 85%), at a lower intensity (50% to 75%). The length of this phase is dependent upon the previous level of competition experience, and the time frame prior to a major competition. The enclosed plan has allotted 6 weeks for the preparatory phase, although, some training phases (ie. strength development) may extend past the preparatory phase into other phases. Physical preparation of judo athletes involves developing the individual's maximal strength capacity. In addition to this, the judo athlete requires an adequate aerobic base, from which anaerobic considerations will be based from. Sport specific training (judo) would involve longer duration spar sessions at a moderate intensity. The majority of the practice time should be focused on refinement of core techniques, with the introduction of selected new techniques. Drills should require the judo athlete to repeat the techniques continuously, several times throughout the week in order to develop a sense of automation during execution of the technique. Mental preparation involves the planning of goals and objectives for the following year, developing stress management and relaxation skills to be used in the subsequent competitions. In summary, the primary focus of the preparatory phase in judo training is physical development and technical mastery of core techniques used during competition.

The Competitive Phase

This phase includes pre-competitive preparation in addition to both general and specific phases of the competition period. The objective of the competitive phase is perfection of all training factors. The contribution of physical preparation is 90% direct (or sport specific tasks) to 10% indirect (general exercises not involving judo tasks). The level of training intensity is increased (80% to 100%), with a reduction in the overall volume of training (50% to 75%). Adequate rest and recovery is essential for optimal physiological adaptation to occur. High intensity training sessions should not exceed more than 3–4 times per week. Emphasis is now on speed, endurance and explosive movements, all of which are characteristics of the requirements for execution of throws. Furthermore, a high volume of lactate training is required in order to present the needed stimulus for peripheral adaptations for lactate tolerance. The focus now changes from technical skill mastery to tactical and strategic plans to be used in specific competition situations and against specific opponents. Mental preparation must incorporate visualization and imagery in order to enhance the simulation training for competition. The main focus is on optimizing physical and mental development for the major competition, leading to peak performance. Bompa (1994) has identified that in general, it may require 7 to 10 competitions to adequately peak for a major event. Specific tactical goals must be made for each competition in order to develop the most effective skills for the major competition. The majority of judo practice time must be spent on competition specific drills. These situations are specific to each individual athlete, and the areas of competition weakness must be regularly rehearsed and practiced in order to overcome potential difficulties. In summary, the competition phase is characteristic of participation in several competitions. Training intensity is maximized, with the focus on competitive situations and tactics. Physical preparation is much lower, with much of the emphasis placed on judo mat work.

The Transition Phase

Following long periods of high volume and intensity training, the elite athlete will require a regeneration period, whereby fatigue, injury, boredom and staleness can be removed via a break from training. During this phase, judo training is at a minimum (between 3 to 5 times per week), and only on a recreation based format. Typical periods last between 3 to 4 weeks, and may be split through the training year. Training activities should include other sporting activities (ie. soccer, outdoor hiking, cycling etc.), which will serve to maintain current physiological adaptations with minimal detraining. In the enclosed annual training chart, two transition periods have been designated, each of which follows the national and world championships. Each transition period allows for a 2 to 3 week period of recovery and regeneration, in order to prepare for further training. Training plans for the upcoming year must also be included during this phase. Goals and objectives for training and competition must be well established, so that both the athlete and coach can work together in accomplishing these parameters.

Strategies for adjusting training in the micro-cycle for judo are largely dependent on the fluctuations of high speed drilling and/or sparring matches (randori). Typically, the higher the intensity of the daily workout, the more randori the athlete participates in. One effective method is to total the number of minutes spent participating in randori. Generally, early in the training year, training programs should incorporate micro-cycles with one peak. Conversely, later in the training year during preparation for peaking, micro-cycles with two or three peaks should be employed. Peak days often involve the double or triple training sessions throughout the day. It is best to conduct supplementary training sessions (conditioning or strength training) earlier in the day (between 9–11 a.m.), and allow a minimum of 6 hours rest until the next session. This method is very effective at increasing training volume, and at integrating other essential training components into the program.

Designing the Judo Training Session

Understanding the energy systems is key to designing any elite training program. In competition judo, the anaerobic system predominates, however, a well developed aerobic base is necessary in order to have the anaerobic system work efficiently. Focus on each systems depends on the competitive season and what the physiological weaknesses the athlete my have. The optimal way to physically prepare the athlete for world class competition is to prepare the athlete for world class training. Each of the following sections will review the energy systems and provide an application to the training room. A sample training session will be presented to demonstrate an approximate schedule for training.

Training the Aerobic System for Judo Specificity

The duration for training the aerobic system usually encompasses 6 to 8 weeks to build a good base, and operates in greater proportion in the latter part of the off season and start of the pre-season. The athlete is required to perform non-specific, continuous activity at a lower intensity (70–85% VO_2) primarily using large muscle groups. Sessions should last 30 to 40 minutes in total duration and be performed at least 3 to 5 times per week (NCCP, 1990). A good example of a workout schedule would be to introduce games as a warm up for this duration (ie: soccer) at the desired intensity. Other strategies would include incorporating dry land training (ie: running, cycling) 3–5 times per week for 6–8 weeks. The aim is to have between 90–120 minutes of straight, relatively uninterrupted physical activity in total per week.

On the other hand, preparing the aerobic system is also done in the judo training room, or 'dojo'. Ideally, sessions should include scrimmage or 'randori' matches at a moderate intensity, but for a longer duration. A good ratio of fighting during this part of the season is 35% ne-waza/25% technique/40% tachi-waza (Beaton, 1998), which will develop fundamental endurance. The Work:Rest ratio is 1:1 or 1:2, with a longer duration of technique performed at a sub-maximal intensity. Therefore, scrimmage sessions may be set at 3–4 x 10 minutes, or 4–6 x 7 minute intervals at a reduced level of intensity. Many coaches will take the time to focus mainly on ground technique or 'ne-waza' in the preparatory phase. This would involve fighting solely on the ground without a break for extended periods of time. As a result, this develops not only good endurance and stamina, but also serves to tactically prepare the athlete by familiarizing them with being exposed to a variety of ground positions

SAMPLE DAILY TRAINING SESSION OUTLINE FOR THE PREPARATORY PERIOD (6-8 WEEKS)

Activity	Duration (minutes)	Description and Recipe
Warm Up	10–15	stretching and calisthenics (HR = 35–55% maximal)
Conditioning	30	dry land conditioning and/or games (HR = 65–75% maximal)
Technique	10–15	Ground: offensive series of combinations (ie: juji gatame-sankakyu jime); Stand: review of counter and combination attacks
Drills	10–15	Uchikomi 6 x 10 (moderate speed); crash pad throw for throw;
Randori	30–45	3–4 x 10 minute or 4–5 x 7 minute rounds (HR = 65–75% maximal) focus should be on repetition of same moves or attacks; each combination to be repeated 4–6 times through a match
Total	90–120	Combinations of each activity can be varied in later sessions.

Sport specific sessions should involve a higher volume and lower intensity formats with focus being on fundamental development. Emphasis should be on developing gross motor movements and overall physical conditioning. Strength training should focus on maximal strength gains of large muscle groups, while mental preparation reflects development of relaxation exercises (refer to strength and mental training section for program specifications). Overall, adequate peaking for major competitions rely on thorough and effective development during the preparatory periods.

Training the Lactate System for Judo Specificity
Training this system would require an interval type format with a Work:Rest of

approximately 1:4 (Cipriano, 1987). This would occur leading up to and during the initial stages of the pre-competitive and competitive seasons; typically lasting eight to twelve weeks in duration (NCCP, 1990). Drill specificity is crucial to maximize adaptation. Therefore, an optimal format would involve situational exercises, where judo athletes are involved in a 'scramble' situation lasting 30 to 60 seconds, which may be repeated 6 to 8 times. For example, each athlete may attempt to defend a certain attack for the first half of the drill, and then attempt to score in the second half of the drill. Another example would involve utilizing a circuit type format for training specific muscle groups. Exercises would consist of maximal work for 30 seconds, which is repeated several times. An example of circuit training is listed in the periodized strength training program, in the muscular endurance phase. Total exercise time is equal to that of a match (5 minutes), and involves maximal exertion with muscle groups involved with judo activity. Recovery should involve sub-maximal work (approximately 40% VO_2) to assist in the removal of lactate from the muscle during the rest phase (Astrand and Rodahl, 1986). Conditioning for this phase may involve 200/100/50 meter repeats at 85–100% maximal heart rate, or repeated hill and/or stair climbing. Any activity can be used insofar as it falls within the specified period of the energy system.

Some sport specific drills that may be used would be repeated entry attacks or 'uchikomi', which require repetitive explosive entry into attacks. These can be done on an incremental basis, with the speed of the technique increasing throughout 10 attacks, or a set high intensity pace for a specific duration (10–30 seconds per set). Other sport specific activity includes multiple partners fighting or 'shark bait', with one athlete remaining on the mat with a new partner changing every 30–60 seconds for 2–6 repeats, depending on the desired intensity level. Included in this format can be situation drilling, where the athlete is placed in a particular precarious position (ie: down a point, in a submission hold etc.) and is pre-set in a disadvantageous position. The match then becomes 'live' and the athletes are required to fight from that particular position for repeated rounds of 10–30 seconds.

Training the Alactate System for Judo Specificity

The ATP-CP system uses creatine phosphate (PCr) to generate intense bursts of action. It is characterized by maximal (100% VO_2) exercise lasting 10 to 15 seconds in duration. The value of this system is its tremendous ability to completely replenish stores after depletion within a period of 2 to 3 minutes of rest (Astrand and Rodahl, 1986). Adaptations that occur involve small increases in the concentration of PCr stores within the muscle. Most of the benefit, however, occurs from an increase in enzyme concentration of CPK (creatine phosphokinase), which will assist with a prolonged use of the ATP-CP system as opposed to a pre-mature use of the lactic system (Cipriano, 1987).

It has been suggested that the ATP-CP system generally requires a period of 2–4 weeks of training for development (Cipriano, 1987). The training period for ATP-CP development is during the competitive season, when judo sparring intensity and is at its maximum (NCCP, 1990). Typical training methodology involves supra-maximal exercise (100 to 110% VO$_2$) lasting 6 to 10 seconds with a recovery of 60 to 100 seconds (Cipriano, 1987). The Work:Rest ratio is then suggested at 1:10, and is repeated 10–15 times throughout the session (NCCP, 1990). High intensity, short duration drills should be performed within the competitive schedule time frame for optimal development of this system. Some examples of sport specific drilling would involve utilizing many of the training drills specified in the lactate system. Others include power uchikomi for 10 seconds, repeating up to 10 to 15 sets. This will develop the explosive nature required when completing an execution of a judo throw. Other examples may include situation drills, where the judo player is placed in the position of an incomplete throw. The athlete then has 10 to 15 seconds to complete the technique or series of techniques at maximal intensity. This cycle of training must encompass high intensity, sport specific situations. Ideal duration of such training should be a frequency of 3 times per week, for a maximum of 3 to 6 weeks in duration.

SAMPLE DAILY TRAINING SESSION OUTLINE FOR THE COMPETITION PERIOD (6–8 WEEKS)

Activity	Duration (minutes)	Description and Recipe
Warm Up	10–15	games (HR = 65–75% maximal)
Conditioning	15	mat circuit system (repeats for total of 5 minutes) involving burpees; lunges; shuttle runs; pushups; leap frog etc. each station for 30 seconds
Technique	15–20	emphasis on grip positions; entrances into attacks and counters
Drills	45	speed uchikomi (10 x 10 sec); grip situations (5–6 x 30 sec); high speed crash pad throwing (10 x 10); line situations (10 x 30 sec); allow for 1–2 minute rests between each set while performing sub-maximal exercise (65%)
Randori	30	30–90 second rounds repeated 6–10 times; intensity maximal (95–100%); use danger mat positions (red zone; behind points)
Total	90–120	

Each judo training session adjusts its respective intensity by performing more or less of randori rounds. Furthermore, each individual session must have a specific goal or focus (ie: defensive position from difficult grips; counter attacks; fighting in the red zone); and all aspects of practice must reflect that focus. Each athlete will focus on differing areas of weakness, however, the main focus of the session will remain the same. In other words, technique, drills and randori need to build on each other throughout the training session to maximize physical and cognitive exposure of competition specific stimuli. Beaton (1998) suggests using a variety of elements in practicing randori ranging from foot and leg attacks only, to multiple combinations (tap and go). The emphasis is on placing the athlete in a situation where they will most likely encounter that particular position. Competition strategies (situations which the athlete will likely encounter during matches) can be employed during the training session for both physical and mental preparation. For example, a popular difficulty athlete's face during competition is fighting in the red zone of the mat. Beaton (1998) suggests incorporating positional changes with attacks to maximize effectiveness when being in the red zone. Essentially, this ensures that the athlete is familiar and comfortable with attacking when being pushed, pulled or held in a pressure time limited situation.

Summary

The physiological basis for training judo athletes is a complex and long-term project. It involves the progressive and systematic adaptation of all three energy systems, within the constraints of the training year. The key to maximizing this adaptation is specificity of training and simulation of competitive situations as closely as possible during the practice session. Regular testing and evaluations should be made to determine both the effectiveness of training and the process of adaptation. This should be implemented at the start and completion of each training phase to provide base values. This will provide a means to initiate amendments in the training program, which will be necessary as the athlete improves in both physical performance and working capacity. Through this approach, the athlete will be able to reach his potential for physical peak performance.

Periodized Strength Training Program for Elite Judo Athletes

Strength training encompasses several different components, and is contingent upon what season or cycle the athlete is actively engaged in. The following program is divided into three main categories, a strength development phase, a power maintenance phase and a muscular endurance phase. The program design involves a cumulative approach, as that each phase is based on what the previous phase has accomplished.

Strength Development Phase

Goal: To improve absolute strength of major muscle groups, specifically, the chest, legs, back and shoulders.

Season: To be executed during the off-season cycle leading into the pre-season cycle.

Method: Program to be repeated 2 to 3x per week, alternating light and heavy sessions for a duration of 6 to 9 weeks. Individual 1 RM (repetition maximum) must be determined in order to each mesocycle load levels. Loading requires increasing the number of reps at 85% 1RM until a base of 6 reps for 6 sets has been completed. Peaking requires increasing the load by 5% from 85% to a maximum of 105%, while reducing the number of reps and sets.

Exercises: Use bench press and leg squats only.

Work/Rest: Complete program starting with level A1 on the first day, and following with A2 on the second day. Continue until week 9 is complete (level I1 and I2). Allow a minimum of 2 to 3 days of active recovery between each sessions. Cross train with conditioning (C) on off days. (See following table for program design).

WEEKLY TRAINING PROGRAM

	Mon	Tue	Wed	Thurs	Fri	Sat	Sun
Week 1	A1	—	C	—	A2	—	—
Week 2	B1	C	—	C	B2	—	—
Week 3	C1	—	C	—	C2	—	—
Week 4	D1	C	—	C	D2	—	—
Week5	E1	—	C	—	E2	—	—
Week 6	F1	C	—	C	F2	—	—
Week 7	G1	—	C	—	G2	—	—
Week 8	H1	C	—	C	H2	—	—
Week 9	I1	—	C	—	I2	—	—

WEEKLY TRAINING LEVELS

A1›
70%	2 x 1
75%	2 x 1
80%	2 x 6

A2›
70%	2 x 1
75%	2 x 1
80%	3 x 6

B1›
70%	2 x 1
75%	2 x 1
80%	2 x 6

B2›
70%	2 x 1
75%	2 x 1
80%	4 x 6

C1›
70%	2 x 1
75%	2 x 1
80%	2 x 6

C2›
70%	2 x 1
75%	2 x 1
80%	5 x 6

D1›
70%	2 x 1
75%	2 x 1
80%	2 x 6

D2›
70%	2 x 1
75%	2 x 1
80%	6 x 6

E1›
70%	2 x 1
75%	2 x 1
80%	2 x 6

E2›
70%	2 x 1
75%	2 x 1
80%	5 x 5

F1›
70%	2 x 1
75%	2 x 1
80%	2 x 6

F2›
70%	2 x 1
75%	2 x 1
90%	2 x 6

G1›
70%	2 x 1
75%	2 x 1
80%	2 x 6

G2›
70%	2 x 1
75%	2 x 1
95%	3 x 3

H1›
70%	2 x 1
75%	2 x 1
80%	2 x 6

H2›
70%	2 x 1
75%	2 x 1
100%	2 x 6

I1›
70%	2 x 1
75%	2 x 1
80%	2 x 6

I2›
70%	2 x 1
75%	2 x 1
105%	1 x 2

Power Maintenance Phase

Goal: To maintain relative strength. To incorporate other exercises and muscle groups. To use the anaerobic alactic system. To train with high velocity movements.

Season: Executed during the pre-season 6–8 weeks prior to competition.

Method: Utilize 6 exercises (all large muscle groups). Repeat program 2 to 3x per week. Use exercises alternately to reduce workout time. Each load is set between 75% to 85% of 1RM. Every 2 weeks, a 1RM attempt should be made in bench press and leg squat. Movements must have explosive concentric movements as fast as possible.

Work/Rest: Perform routine 2x per week with 2–3 days rest between each training session. Maintain conditioning on the off days. Supplemental exercises may be done during the conditioning workout. Total time for each session should not exceed 60 minutes duration. Recovery time between each set should not exceed 2 minutes. Each set should require approximately 10 to 15 seconds of work. Each training session should be completed a minimum of 5–6 hours prior to practice.

A ›   POWER MAINTENANCE EXERCISES

	Exercises:	Sets	Reps
1.	Bench Press	4–6	6–8
2.	Leg Squat	4–6	8–10
3.	Power Cleans	4–6	6–8
4.	Bent Over Rows	4–6	6–8
5.	Upright Rows	4–6	6–8
6.	Shoulder Press	4–6	8–10

B ›   SUPPLIMENTAL POWER MAINTENANCE EXERCISES

	Exercises:	Sets	Reps
1.	Chin Ups	3–4	15–25
2.	Dips	3–4	15–25
3.	Sit Ups (incline)	3–4	20–30
4.	Back Extensions	3–4	20–30

1. Bench Press

2. Leg Squat

3. Power Cleans

4. Bent Over Rows

5. Upright Rows

6. Shoulder Press

1. Chin Ups

2. Dips

3. Sit Ups (incline)

4. Back Extensions

Muscular Endurance Phase

Goal: To develop tolerance to lactic acid fatigue. To train the anaerobic lactic energy system. To focus on high intensity, high velocity exertion similar to competitive situations. To incorporate plyometric training.

Season: To be initiated during the competitive season, for a duration of 4 to 6 weeks in length.

Method: The circuit is to be performed 2x per training session for a total time of 5 minutes. Circuits are to be performed every other day for 3 days per week. Sessions to be held in the morning, with a minimum of 5–6 hours prior to practice. All of the exercises are to be done at maximum intensity as fast as possible. This is essential in order to establish muscle hypoxia, which is the necessary stimulus for anaerobic training adaptation.

Exercises: Warm-up activity of cycling, rope jumping etc. at sub-maximal heart rate for 5 minutes. Stretch the muscle groups involved in the circuit.

Work/Rest: Each station lasts 30 seconds of work with very low resistance. Their is no rest between each station, only the time it takes (5 sec.) to move to the following station. Total exercise time is 2.5 minutes, which is repeated twice for a total of 5 minutes. Each muscle groups rests 120 sec. before it is repeated the second time. A total of 10 to 15 minutes of rest should be included between each circuit repeat. During this time, mild aerobic activity is suggested to aid in the removal of lactic acid from the muscles. Only perform 2–3 circuits per training session.

C › CIRCUIT TRAINING EXERCISES

	Exercises:	*Time*
1.	Bent Over Rows	30 sec.
2.	Trunk Twists (with weight)	30 sec.
3.	Back Extensions	30 sec.
4.	Jumping Squats	30 sec.
5.	Bench Press	30 sec.
	Total:	**150 sec.**

Repeat steps 1 through 5 with no rest once only.

1. Bent Over Rows

2. Trunk Twists (with weight)

3. Back Extensions

4. Jumping Squats

5. Bench Press

Mental Preparation Program

Mental training is a crucial component of developing successful athletes. Through mental preparation, the athlete is focused and prepared for the dynamics of competition. The following will examine a periodized plan of mental preparation. The majority of the focus is on the development and completion of pre-set goals and objectives. Through establishing a goal program, the athlete will be able to systematically develop mental skills necessary for optimal competitive mental performance. The improvement in mental development will aid in execution of physical skills, as well as an overall improvement in self-confidence and self-efficacy. Refer to the 'Annual Training Plan' to see examples of where to incorporate the mental training phases. These phases are congruent with physical preparation within the same macro-cycle. Consequently, mental training is designed to enhance physical training in order to extract the athlete's full potential from the practice session.

This program will be directed towards the mental development of a national level judo athlete preparing for the world championships. Techniques utilized were adopted from Suinn (1986). The plan will be divided into four components: technical, tactical, strategical and peak. Each of these stages encompasses specific mental training techniques, which will include objectives, exercises and evaluations. This section will conclude with a review of some of the benefits achieved through a goal setting program, independent of performance outcome.

Technical Phase: Stress Management and Relaxation

Objective: To promote relaxation and recovery from physical mental stress. Develop skills to manage competitive anxieties. To reduce heart rate values immediately prior to and after competition matches.

Exercise: To perform relaxation techniques at the completion of training sessions, with the assistance of audio tapes. To complete questionnaires which focus on emotional status before competitive situations. To monitor heart rate response and use biofeedback along with verbal cues as a means in effectively lowering heart rate. To perform exercises for 20 minute sessions, 2x per week. Then gradually reduce sessions by 5 minutes to develop a short form, which can be used for competitive situations.

Evaluation: Compare pre and post phase heart rate recovery values prior to and after competitive matches. Compare pre and post phase self reports on anxiety levels.

Key is to apply techniques in competitive situations, such as weekly matches.

General Instructions: Indicate how much stress you have experienced in each of the following areas when compared to the amount you usually experience. Total your scores and record weekly to monitor fluctuations in training throughout the year.

Reference: NCCP (1990)

	More		Average		Less
a) Training	1	2	3	4	5
b) Academics	1	2	3	4	5
c) Family	1	2	3	4	5
d) Social	1	2	3	4	5
e) Financial	1	2	3	4	5
f) From Self	1	2	3	4	5

Tactical Phase: Visualization and Imagery

Objectives: To review status on core techniques, and identify weaknesses in execution of techniques. To improve technical performance and skill. To improve reaction time, and frequency of successfully executed technique during a competitive situation.

Exercise: Perform video analysis of the individual during competitive situations executing the problem technique. Increase frequency of technical drills to improve reaction times. Perform visualization exercises prior to matches during training sessions. Focus is to be on speed, intensity and success of technique. Individual to provide mental pictures of themselves performing technique a minimum of 3x per week, for 10 minutes each.

Evaluation: Test post phase reaction times performing trained technique to determine if imagery or visualization had any effect. Critique post phase competition video-tape to observe any increase in both frequency and success of problem technique.

Strategical Phase: Mental Rehearsal

Objectives: To focus on tactics for both offensive and defensive situations against specific opponents. To mentally prepare for expectations of the upcoming competitive environment. To employ specific strategies for competition, and rehearse in a simulated competitive situation.

Exercise: To critique specific techniques and strategies employed by opponents via video analysis. Practice mental rehearsal of competitive strategies during the training session. Perform exercises at least 2x per week for 15 minute sessions. Observe video, and re-create situations expected to be encountered with opponents. Have athletes complete a self report questionnaire on level of self confidence in competitive situations involving different opponents.

Evaluation: Evaluate questionnaire for improvements in level of self-confidence at the completion of this phase. Observe behaviour during training sessions for changes in frequency of initiating attacks, commitment in completing technique, and other overt signs of improved level of confidence.

Peak Phase: Energy Control and Focusing

Objective: To incorporate all 3 previous components in simulated competitive situations. To determine optimal excitation and activation levels for competitive performance. To focus on the 'winning feeling', and other positive emotions associated with successful competitive experiences.

Exercise: Have individuals complete an evaluation outlining specific emotional and physical cues associated with ideal competitive experiences. Integrate thought control and emotional control during training sessions prior to simulated competiton.

Evaluation: Use questionnaire to determine optimal activation and excitation levels. Require athletes to practice these techniques to either increase or decrease activation levels to meet within the optimal range. Observe behaviour during training to objectively evaluate whether the individual is aware of their motivational cues, and are using them effectively.

Each phase takes place over a different month. Therefore, there are approximately four weeks to train each skill. The phases reflect the periodized physical training program, therefore providing a complete plan. The obvious result is an increase in competitive performance, however, other benefits may incur as well. Through the completion of the program, the individual will experience satisfaction in the successful accomplishment of a task. Furthermore, the athlete will hopefully obtain greater self-confidence and self efficacy with respect to competitive situations. The techniques presented offer methods to manage difficulties experienced by competitors, as well as motivational techniques. Each objective has been presented as challenging, just out of reach, and retains a great deal of specificity to the sport.

Summary

Most elite training programs attempt to induce short-term cycles of intensive training in order to maximize training adaptations, however, if not monitored regularly, these training sessions can predispose the athlete to states of overtraining. Several parameters can be used in the assessment and evaluation of training progression. It does appear that a multi-faceted approach is optimal in determining whether overtraining has taken place. Studies have demonstrated that several factors often determine subsequent ones. In other words, the biology of overtraining can be observed in physiological, psychological and performance evaluations. Regular testing and monitoring of training loads throughout the season is the only way to assess the success of the training program. Self evaluation is a reliable method of assessing whether the athlete is approaching a state of overtraining. The coach is well advised to develop a simple chart that athlete can use to monitor their daily moods and feeling of fatigue and recovery.

Planning the training year of an elite athlete involves an awareness of the physical, technical and psychological demands of the sport. The most important task is the ability to evenly distribute the components of training so as to maximize the benefits and/or adaptations. It is important to note that training elite individuals is a long-term process, involving years of preparation. Bompa (1994) has suggested that it requires at least 6 to 8 years to develop an elite athlete. Furthermore, the first half of this period is primarily concerned with the physical development of the athlete to withstand the rigours of training. The later half is then spent focusing and refining the intricate features of high performance sport.

The elite coach, must have an appreciation of the scientific nature to which the athlete exists within the sport. This book was designed with that objective and purpose in mind. The benefit of understanding physiological landmarks of the athlete is the ability to prescribe individual training plans for athletes developing at different rates. Unfortunately, judo is a relatively new sport, which has yet to be fully examined by the scientific community, although the judo coach can make use of this science based information in order to validate and quantify current and future training regimes. Rather than present a step by step approach to training, this book examined and quantified the physical demands of elite judo performance. It is hoped that the material presented in this book may serve as a means for that purpose to be used by both the high performance coach and athlete in their pursuit of sport excellence.

Annual Training Plan   Year: 1992 – 1993   Prepared by Wayland Pulkkinen

REFERENCES

ACEVEDO, E.O., H. GOLDFARB. (1989). Increased training intensity effects on plasma lactate, ventilatory threshold, and endurance. *Medicine and Science in Sports and Exercise.* 21 (5): 563–568.

ASTRAND P., K RODAHL. (1986). Textbook of work physiology. *Physiological bases of exercise.* McGraw Hill Book Company. New York.

BANFI, G., M. MARINELLI, G.S. ROI, V. AGAPE. (1993). Usefulness of free testosterone/cortisol ratio during a season of elite speed skating athletes. *International Journal of Sports Medicine.* 14 (7): 373–379.

BEATON, E. (1998). Junior National Team's Basic Competition Peaking and Development Model & Technical Tip: *Developing Good Ashi-Waza.* Unpublished document. Judo Saskatchewan.

BOMPA, T.O. (1994). *Theory and methodology of training: the key to athletic performance. (3rd edition).* Dubuque, Iowa: Kendall Hunt.

BOONE, J.B. JR., T. SHERRADEN, K. PIERZCHALA, R. BERGER, G.R. VAN LOON. (1992). Plasma metenkephalin and catecholamine responses to intense exercise in humans. *Journal of Applied Physiology.* 73 (1): 388–392.

BROOKS G.A., T.D. FAHEY. (1985). *Exercise Physiology: Human bioenergentics and its applications.* Macmillan Publishing Company, New York.

BROUSSE, M., D. MATSUMOTO. (1999). *Judo: A Sport and A Way of Life.* International Judo Federation. Seoul.

BROWNELL, K.D., S. NELSON-STEEN, J. WILMORE. (1987). Weight regulation and practices in athletes: analysis of metabolic and health effects. *Medicine and Science in Sports and Exercise.* 19 (6): 546–545.

BUDGET, R. (1990). Overtraining syndrome. *British Journal of Sports Medicine.* 24 (4).

BURGE, C.M., M.F. CAREY, W.R. PAYNE. (1993). Rowing performance, fluid balance and metabolic function following dehydration and rehydration. *Medicine and Science in Sports and Exercise.* 25 (12): 1358–1364.

CALLISTER, R., S.J. FLECK, G.A. DUDLEY. (1990). Physiological and performance responses to overtraining in elite judo athletes. *Medicine and Science in Sports and Exercise.* 22 (6): 816–824.

CALLISTER, R., R.S. STARON, S.J. FLECK, P. TESCH, G.A.DUDLEY. (1991). Physiological characteristics of elite judo athletes. *International Journal of Sports Medicine.* 12 (2): 196–203.

CIPRIANO, N., T.M.K. SONG. (1984). Effects of seasonal training on physical and physiological function on elite varsity wrestlers. *The Journal of Sports Medicine and Physical Fitness.* 24 (2): 123–130.

CIPRIANO, N. (1987). Physical conditioning principles and protocols for amateur freestyle wrestling. *National Strength and Conditioning Association Journal.* 9 (4): 46–50.

CIPRIANO, N. (1993). Technical-tactical analysis of free-style wrestling. *Journal of Strength and Conditioning Research.* 7 (3): 133–140.

COHN, P.J. (1991). An exploratory study on peak performance in golf. *The Sport Psychologist.* 5: 1–14.

COLES, D. (1999). *Making the Weight: Judoka's Practices.* Unpublished graduate thesis for the degree Master of Science (Sport and Exercise Science). University of Wales Institute, Cardiff.

DAVIDSON, R.L., J.D. ROBERTSON, R.J. MAUGHAN. (1986). Hematological changes due to triathalon competition. *British Journal of Sports Medicine.* 20 (4): 159–156.

DE CREE, C., R. LEWIN, A. BARROS. (1995). Hypoestrogenemia and rhabdomyelysis (myoglobinuria) in the female judoist: a new worrying phenomenon? *Journal of Clinical Endcrinology and Metabolism.* 80 (12):3639–3646.

DESCHENES, M., W. KRAEMER. (1989). The biochemical basis of muscular fatigue. *National Strength and Conditioning Journal.* 11 (6): 41–43.

FISCHER, R. (1981). *The complete training guide for judo.* Toronto: Ontario Ministry of Culture and Recreation.

FOGELHOLM, G., R. KOSKINEN, J. LAAKSO, T. RANKINEN, I. RUOKONEN. (1993). Gradual and rapid weight loss: effects on nutrition and performance in male athletes. *Medicine and Science in Sports and Exercise.* 25 (3): 371–377.

FRY, R.W., A.R. MORTON, P. GARCIA-WEBB, G.P. CRAWFORD, D. KEAST. (1992). Biological responses to overload training in endurance sports. *European Journal of Applied Physiology.* 64 (4): 335–344.

FRY, R.W., A. MORTON, AND D. KEAST. (1992). Periodization and the prevention of overtraining. *Canadian Journal of Sport Sciences.* 17 (3): 241–248.

FRY, R.W., A.R. MORTON, P. GARCIA-WEBB, D. KEAST. (1991). Monitoring exercise stress by changes in metabolic and hormonal responses over a 24 hour period. *European Journal of Applied Physiology.* 63 (3–4): 228–234.

GAESSER, G.A. (1994). Influence of endurance training and catecholamines on exercise VO_2 response. *Medicine and Science in Sports and Exercise.* 26 (11): 1341–1346.

GAMES OF THE XXV OLYMPIAD: BARCELONA 1992. (1992). Results: Judo. (Results of the Judo Competition). Edition: *COOB '92.* Pl. de la Font Magicia, 08038 Barcelona: Printer Industria Grafica,

GARFIELD, C.A. (1984). *Peak performance: mental training techniques of the world's greatest athletes.* New York: Warner Books Inc.

GILMAN, M.B., C.L. WELLS. (1993). The use of heart rates to monitor exercise intensity in relation to metabolic variables. *International Journal of Sports Medicine.* 14: 339–344.

GOULD, D., M. WEISS, R. WEINBERG. (1981). Psychological characteristics of successful and non-successful big ten wrestlers. *Journal of Sport Psychology.* 3: 69–81.

HACKNEY, A.C. (1989). Endurance training and testosterone levels. *Sports Medicine.* 8 (2): 117–127.

HAKKINEN, K., K.L. KESKINEN, M. ALEN, P.V. KOMI, H. KAUHANEN. (1989). Serum hormone concentrations during prolonged training in elite endurance trained and strength trained athletes. *The European Journal of Applied Physiology.* 59: 233–238.

HEYMAN, S.R. (1982). Comparisons of successful and unsuccessful competitors: a reconsideration of methodological questions data. *Journal of Sport Psychology.* 4: 295–300.

HIGHEN, P.S., B.B. BENNETT. (1983). Elite divers and wrestlers: a comparison between open and closed skill athletes. *Journal of Sport Psychology.* 5: 390–409.

HOLDEN, S., H. MACRAE, S.C. DENNIS, A.N. BOSCH, T.D. NOAKES. (1992). Effects of training on lactate production and removal during progressive exercise in humans. *Journal of Applied Physiology.* 72 (5): 1649–1656.

HOOPER, S.L., L.T. MACKINNON, R.D. GORDON, A.W. BACHMANN. (1993). Hormonal responses of elite swimmers to overtraining. *Medicine and Science in Sports and Exercise.* 25 (6):741–747.

HOOPER, S.L., L.T. MACKINNON, A. HOWARD, R.D. GORDON, A.W. BACHMANN. (1995). Markers for monitoring overtraining and recovery. *Medicine and Science in Sports and Exercise.* 27 (1): 106–112.

HORSWILL, C.A, J.R. SCOTT, R.W. DICK, J. HAYES. (1994). Influence of rapid weight gain after the weigh-in on success in collegiate wrestlers. *Medicine and Science in Sports and Exercise.* 26 (9): 1290–1294.

HORSWILL, C.A., J.E. MILLER, J.R. SCOTT, C.M. SMITH, G. WELK, P. VAN HANDEL. (1992). Anaerobic and aerobic power in arms and legs of elite senior wrestlers. *International Journal of Sports Medicine.* 13 (8): 558–561.

HOUMARD, J.A., B.K. SCOTT, C.L. JUSTICE, T.C. CHENIER. (1994). The effects of taper on performance in distance runners. *Medicine and Science in Sports and Exercise.* 26 (4)624–631.

HOUMARD, J.A. (1991). Impact of reduced training performance in endurance athletes. *Sports Medicine.* 12 (6): 380–393.

INOKUMA, I., N. SATO. (1986). *Best Judo.* Kodansha International Limited. Tokyo.

JACOBS, I. (1986). Blood lactate implications for training and sports performance. *Sports Medicine.* 3: 10–25.

KANEKO, M., M. IWATA, S. TOMIOKA. (1978). Studies on the Oxygen Uptake and Heart Rate During Judo Practice. *Bulletin of the Association for the Scientific Studies on Judo, Kodokan.* (5): 19–30.

KIBLER, W.B., T.J. CHANDLER, E.S. STRACENER. (1992). Musculoskeletal adaptations and injuries due to overtraining. *Exercise and Sport Science Review.* 20: 99–126.

KINGSBURY, K.J., L. KAY, M. HJELM. (1998). Contrasting plasma free amino acid patterns in elite athletes: association with fatigue and infection. *British Journal of Sports Medicine.* 32 (1): 25–32.

KLINZING, J.E., W. KARPOWICZ. (1986). The effects of rapid weight loss and rehydration on a wrestling performance test. *Journal of Sports Medicine and Physical Fitness.* 26: 149–156.

KOUTEDAKIS, Y., A. RAAFAT, N.C.C. SHARP, M.N. ROSMARIN, M.J. BEARD, S.W. ROBBINS. (1993). Serum enzyme activities in individuals with different levels of physical fitness. *The Journal of Sports Medicine and Physical Fitness.* 33: 252–257.

KOUTEDAKIS, Y.R., R. BUDGET, L. FAULMANN. (1990). Rest in under performing elite competitors. *British Journal of Sports Medicine.* 24 (4): 248–252.

KUIPERS, H., H.A. KEIZER. (1988). Overtraining in elite athletes: a review and directions for the future. *Sports Medicine.* 6: 79–92.

LEHMANN, M., H.H. DICKHUTH, G.GENDRISCH, W. LAZAR, M. KAMINSKI, J.F. ARAMENDI, E. PETERKE, W. WIELAND, J. KEUL. (1991). Training/overtraining. A prospective, experimental study with experienced middle and long distance runners. *International Journal of Sports Medicine.* 12 : 444–452.

LEHMANN, M., C. FOSTER, J. KEUL. (1993). Overtraining in endurance athletes: a brief review. *Medicine and Science in Sports and Exercise.* 25 (7): 854–862.43.

LITTLE, N.G. (1991). Physical performance attributes of junior and senior women, juvenile, junior, and senior men judokas. *Journal of Sports Medicine and Physical Fitness.* 31 (4): 510–520.

MACDOUGALL, J.D., H.A. WENGER, H.J. GREEN. (1992). *Physiological testing of the high-performance athlete (2nd ed.)*. Champaign, Illinois: Human Kinetics Books.

MARTENS, R. (1988). *Coaches Guide to Sports Psychology.* Champaign, Illinois: Human Kinetics Books.

MACKINNON, L.T., S. HOOPER. (1991). Overtraining. *National Sports Research Program.* Australia. No. 26.

MALCZEWSKA, J., W. BLACH, R. STUPNIKI. (2000). The effects of physical exercise on the concentrations of ferritin and transferrin receptor in plasma of female judoists. *International Journal of Sports Medicine.* 21 (3): 175–179.

MARCINIK, E.J., J. POTTS, G. SCHLABACH, S. WILL, P. DAWSON, B.F. HURLEY. (1991). Effects of strength training on lactate threshold and endurance performance. *Medicine and Science in Sports and Exercise.* 23 (6): 739–743.

MATSUMOTO, Y., O. SHINKICHI, Y. FURUTA, T. OGATA. (1978). Studies in the Training of Judoists, Investigation in the Effect of Training General Endurance. *Bulletin of the Association for the Scientific Studies on Judo, Kodokan.* (5): 7–17.

MAZZEO, R.S., P. MARSHALL. (1989). Influence of plasma catecholamines on the lactate threshold during graded exercise. *Journal of Applied Physiology.* 67 (4): 1319–1322.

MCLELLAN, T.M., I. JACOBS. (1989). Active recovery, endurance training, and the calculation of the individual anaerobic threshold. *Medicine and Science in Sports and Exercise.* 21 (5): 586–592.

MCLELLAN, T.M., K.S.Y. CHEUNG, I. JACOBS. (1991). Incremental test protocol, recovery mode and the individual anaerobic threshold. *International Journal of Sports Medicine.* 12 (2): 190–195.49.

MICKIEWICZ, G., J. STARCZEWSKA, L. BORKOWSKI. (1987). *Physiological characteristics of Polish national team judoists in 1981–1987.* Department of Physiology. Institute of Sport: Warsaw, Poland.

MNATZAKIAN, P.A., P. VACCARO. (1986). The effects of dehydration and rehydration in wrestlers. *American Corrective Therapy Journal.* 40 (1): 17–21.

MOGNONI, P., M.D. SIRTORI, F. LORENZELLI, P. CERRETELLI. (1990). Physiological responses during prolonged exercise at the power output corresponding to the blood lactate threshold. *The European Journal of Applied Physiology.* 60: 239–243.

MORGAN, W.P., J.S. BROWN, J.S. RAGLIN, P.J. O'CONNOR, K.A. ELLICKSON. (1987). Psychological monitoring of overtraining and staleness. *British Journal of Sports Medicine.* 21 (3): 107–114.

NATIONAL COACHING CERTIFICATION PROGRAMME (NCCP). (1990). *Level III: judo technical manual.* Gloucester, Ontario: Judo Canada.

NEUFER, P.D. (1989). The effect of detraining and reduced training on the physiological adaptations to aerobic exercise training. *Sports Medicine.* 8 (5): 302–321.52.

NEWHOUSE, I. (1984). *Overtraining*. Unpublished manuscript. University of British Columbia. 1–42.

ORLICK, T. AND J. PARTINGTON. (1986). Mental links to excellence. *The Sports Psychologist*. 2: 105–130.

OSTERUD, B., J.O. OLSEN, L. WILSGARD. (1989). Effect of strenuous exercise on blood monocytes and their relation to coagulation. *Medicine and Science in Sports and Exercise*. 21 (4): 374–378.

OYONO-ENGUELLE, A. HEITZ, J. MARBACH, C. OTT, M. GARTNER, A. PAPE, J.C. VOLLMER, H. FREUND. (1990). Blood lactate during constant load exercise at aerobic and anaerobic thresholds. *The European Journal of Applied Physiology*. 60: 321–330.

PAAVOLAINEN, L., K. HAKKINEN, H. RUSKO. (1991). Effects of explosive type strength training on physical performance characteristics in cross-country skiers. *The European Journal of Applied Physiology*. 62: 251–255.

PATE, R.R., J.D. BRANCH. (1992). Training for endurance sport. *Medicine and Science in Sports and Exercise*. 24 (9): s340–s343.

PILARDEAU, P.A., F. LAVIE, J. VAYSSE, M. GARNIER, P. HARICHAUX, J.N. MARGO, M.T. CHALUMEAU. (1988). Effect of different work loads on sweat production and composition in man. *The Journal of Sports Medicine and Physical Fitness*. 28 (3): 247–253.

PIVARNIK, J.M., J. WILKERSON. (1988). Recovery metabolism and thermoregulation of endurance trained and heat acclimatized men. *The Journal of Sports Medicine and Physical Fitness*. 28 (4): 375–380.

PULKKINEN, W.J. (1992). *Physical performance tests in varsity wrestlers*. (unpublished graduate document for physical education 5071). Thunder Bay, Ontario: Lakehead University.

PULKKINEN, W.J. (1989). *Training principles for judo*. (unpublished undergraduate document for physical education 3M6). Hamilton, Ontario: McMaster University.

ROSS, J.H., E.C. ATTWOOD. (1984). Severe repetitive exercise and hematological status. *Post Graduate Medical Journal*. 60: 454–457.

SALE, D.G. AND J.D. MACDOUGALL. (1981). Specificity in strength training: a review for the coach and athlete. *Science Periodical On Research and Technology in Sport*. Coaching Association of Canada.

SALVADORA, A., F. SUAY, S. MARTINEZ-SANCHIS, V.M. SIMON, P.F. BRAIN. (1999). Correlating testosterone and fighting in male participants in judo contests. *Physiological Behaviour*. 68 (1-2): 205–209.

SAPSE, A.T. (1984). Stress, cortisol, interferon and 'stress' diseases. *Medical Hypotheses*. 13: 31–44.

SAWKA, M.N., A. YOUNG, R. FRANCESCONI, S. MUZA, K. PANDOLF. (1985). Thermoregulatory and blood responses during exercise at graded hypohydration levels. *Journal of Applied Physiology*. 59: 1394–1401.

SELYE, H. (1956). *The stress of life.* New York: McGraw-Hill Book Co.

SHEPLEY, B., J.D. MACDOUGALL, N. CIPRIANO, J.R. SUTTON, M.A. TARNOPOLSKY, G, COATES. (1992). Physiological effects of tapering in highly trained athletes. *Journal of Applied Physiology.* 2 (2): 706–711.

SHARP, N.C., Y. KOUTEDAKIS. (1987). Anaerobic power and capacity measurements of the upper body in elite judo players, gymnasts and rowers. *The Australian Journal of Science and Medicine in Sport.* 19 (3): 9–13.

SIKORSKI, W., G. MICKIEWICZ, B. MAOLE, C. LASKA. (1987). *Structure of the contest and work capacity of the judoist.* Polish Judo Association. Institute of Sport: Warsaw, Poland.

SILANIKOVE, N. (1994). The struggle to maintain hydration and osmoregulation in animals experiencing severe dehydration and rapid rehydration: the story of ruminants. *Experimental Physiology.* 79: 281–300.

SONG, T.M.K. (1980). *Flexibility and strength for wrestling. A Scientific Approach to Wrestling.* Canadian Amateur Wrestling Association. 13–22.

SPRYNAROVA, S., A. BASS, E. MACKOVA, K. VONDRA, V. VITEK, J. TEISINGER, M. MALKOVSKA. (1980). Changes in maximal aerobic power, aerobic capacity, and muscle enzyme activities at two stages of the annual training cycle in ski runners. *The European Journal of Applied Physiology.* 44: 17–23.

STEGMANN, H., W. KINDERMANN, A. SCHNABEL. (1982). Lactate kinetics and the individual anaerobic threshold. *International Journal of Sports Medicine.* 2: 160–165.

STRAY-GUNDERSEN, J. (1990). Overtraining: markers associated with over-training. In Casey, M.J.(ed.); *Winter Sports Medicine.* Philadelphia, PA: F.A. Davis Company. 72–77.

SUAY, S., A. SALVADORA, A., E. GONZALEZ-BONO, C. SANCHIS, M. MARTINEZ, M. MARTINEZ-SANCHIS, V.M. SIMON, J.B. MONTORO (1999). Effects of competition and its outcome on serum testosterone, cortisol and prolactin. *Psychoneuroendocrinology.* 24 (5): 551–566.

SUINN, R.M. (1986). *Seven steps to peak performance.* Toronto, Ontario: Hans Huber Publishing.

SYNDER, A.C., A.E. JEUKENDRUP, M.K.C. HESSELINK, H. KUIPERS, C. FOSTER. (1992). A physiological/psychological indicator of over-reaching during intensive training. *International Journal of Sports Medicine.* 14 (1): 29–32.

TAKAHASHI, R. (1992). Power training for judo: plyometric training with medicine balls. *National Strength and Conditioning Association Journal.* 14 (2): 66–71.

TARNOPOLSKY, M.A., N. CIPRIANO, C. WOODCROFT, W.J. PULKKINEN, D. ROBINSON, J. HENDERSON, J.D. MACDOUGALL. (1996). The effects of rapid weight loss and wrestling on muscle glycogen concentration. *Clinical Journal of Sport Medicine.* 6: 78–84.

TAYLOR, A.W., L. BRASSARD. (1981). A physiological profile of the Canadian judo team. *Journal of Sports Medicine and Physical Fitness.* 21: 160–164.

THOMAS, S., M.H. COX, Y.M. LEGAL, H.K. SMITH, T.J. VERDE. (1989). Physiological profiles of the Canadian national judo team. *Canadian Journal of Sport Science.* 14 (3): 142–147.

TSAI, L., C. JOHANSSON, A. POUSETTE, R. TEGELMAN, K. CARLSTROM, P. HEMMINGSSON. (1991). Cortisol and androgen concentrations in female and male elite endurance athletes in relation to physical activity. *The European Journal of Applied Physiology.* 63: 308–311.79.

UNDERWOOD, B. (1986). *Application of physiology to training principles in endurance and power sports.* United States Olympic Committee Coaches College.

URHAUSEN, A., B. COEN, B. WEILER, W. KINDERMANN. (1993). Individual anaerobic threshold and maximum lactate steady state. *International Journal of Sports Medicine.* 14 (3): 134–139.

VERKHOSHANSKY, Y.V., V.V. LAZAREV. (1989). Principles of planning speed and strength/speed endurance training in sports. *National Strength Conditioning Association Journal.* 11 (2): 58–61.

VOS, N.N., A.C. FRY, W.J. KRAEMER. (1992). The role of anaerobic exercise in overtraining. *National Strength Conditioning Association Journal.* 14 (3): 74–79.

WHITNEY, E. N., E. HAMILTON, S. ROLFES. (1990). *Understanding Nutrition.* (5th edition). West Publishing Company, St. Paul, Minnesota.

WOLACH, B., B. FALK, R. VAVRIELI, E. KODESH, A. ELIAKIM. (2000). Neutrophil function response to aerobic and anaerobic exercise in female judoka and untrained subjects. *British Journal of Sports Medicine.* 34 (1): 23–28.

ABOUT THE AUTHOR

Wayland J. Pulkkinen has been practicing judo for over 25 years, and is a registered 4th degree black belt in Kodokan Judo. He is a former member of the Canadian National Judo Team, and has competed and participated in many international judo competitions and training camps throughout his athletic career. In addition, Mr. Pulkkinen is a former national level competitive freestyle wrestler, who competed for two different university and club teams.

Wayland J. Pulkkinen

His education includes a Bachelor of Physical Education (McMaster University), a Master of Science in Applied Sport Science and Coaching (Lakehead University), and academic credit courses in Health Studies (University of Waterloo).

Mr. Pulkkinen is a fully certified Level 3 coach under the National Coaching Certification Program (N.C.C.P.) in both judo and wrestling, and also has completed several Level 4 and Level 5 N.C.C.P. tasks towards certification. He is a former chair of the provincial program for Judo Ontario, as well as a course conductor and presenter for N.C.C.P. courses.

He has presented at academic and coaching conferences, in addition to being published in both academic and non-academic journals, and he continues to present and conduct educational seminars and workshops in the sport science and health fields.

At present, Mr. Pulkkinen is currently the president and director of Pulkinetics Health Services Inc., which is based in Guelph, Ontario, Canada. The company provides ergonomic, health and rehabilitation assessments and services to both the private and corporate sectors.

His professional memberships and designations include: Certfied Kinesiologist (C.K.) with the Ontario Kinesiology Association, and Charter Professional Coach (Ch.P.C.) with the Canadian Professional Coaches Association.

He continues to teach and practice judo and jujutsu, and is active in ice hockey and running within Guelph and the surrounding communities.

Wayland Pulkkinen throwing an opponent in the 1991 Canada Cup tournament.